Don't Forget To Look Up

Don't Forget To Look Up

A Christian's Guide to Overcoming Anxiety and Panic Attacks

written by
Angela K. Brittain

edited by
Barbara Tschantz

BRITTAIN
COMMUNICATIONS

North Canton, Ohio

Unless otherwise noted all scripture references are from the
King James Version.

Includes bibliographical references and index.

ISBN 0-9662003-0-6
Library of Congress Catalog Card Number: 97-94922

ATTENTION ORGANIZATIONS AND COUNSELING CENTERS:

Quantity discounts are available on bulk purchases of this book for
educational purposes or fund raising. Special books or book
excerpts can also be created to fit specific needs. For information,
please contact Brittain Communications, P.O. Box 2567,
North Canton, Ohio, 44720.

Dedication

This book is dedicated to my mother-in-law, the late Beverly French. I didn't have the privilege of knowing her for very long, but while I did she expressed to me the importance of enjoying life. She told me that when people near the end of their lives, they don't wish they would have spent more time at the office or kept a cleaner house. Instead, they wish they'd have relaxed a little and enjoyed their children and families. And I'm trying to do just that, Bev. We'll see you when we get to Heaven!

I would like to dedicate the fourth printing of this title to Jim Starcher, "Opa." My husband, son and I had the privilege of living beside Jim and his family for eight years. Opa was more than a neighbor, he was a friend and father figure. On January 10, 2002, after a short, courageous bout with cancer, Opa began his new life with Jesus in Heaven. We sure do miss him down here in this life, but we know we will be rejoicing with him in the next!

Acknowledgements

With great thanks I want to acknowledge:

My parents, Ken and Peg Roberts, who raised me in the nurture and admonition of the Lord. Without them, I don't know where I'd be today.

My wonderful husband, Randy, whose love and understanding have helped me find out what it really means to enjoy life.

My sister, Dana, for being a friend and helping with the process of birthing this book.

My best friend, Kelly Hostetler, who has stood by me through thick and thin for the past 22 years and who helps me keep my focus on the Lord.

My friend and colleague, Barbara Tschantz, for her meticulous editing that helped put the finishing touches on this book.

My pastors and friends, Dr. C. Herschel and Rev. M. Dana Gammill, whose counseling, prayers and patience were priceless.

My doctors, Rajdev Grewal, M.D., and Massood R. Babai, M.D., for their medical expertise in helping me overcome panic disorder.

My son, Luke, for giving me new meaning in life.

And finally, my Father God, for loving me too much to leave me the way I was.

When I originally wrote and published "Don't Forget To Look Up," I never dreamed it would be used to the extent that it has been to help set people free from anxiety and panic disorders. The Lord has brought new people into my life who have helped further its reach. For example, Gayle Harrold and Luis LaCourt, from Rivertree Christian Church, who were vital in facilitating our first support group; Mel Cruzado, who created the "overcomepanic" website; and countless others who have been instrumental in what has become a true ministry. I can't wait to see what God has planned next!

Contents

Preface

The purpose of this book is to help those who suffer from anxiety and panic attacks. When I was diagnosed with panic disorder in the late 1980s, I searched the shelves of Christian stores for books on the subject. Much to my dismay, I found books that dealt with anxiety, depression and worry, but none that dealt specifically with panic attacks. Since then, it has been my goal to write a book that did so. This book tells readers how to cope with symptoms of anxiety and panic and eventually remain calm, even when the storms of life begin to rage.

Don't Forget To Look Up, the title of this book, has a two-fold meaning. First, it reminds the reader to look to our Heavenly Father during times of trial and tribulation. Second, it stresses to the person suffering from anxiety and panic to "take a break." Instead of racing head-down, full speed ahead, everyone needs to look up once in a while, or life will pass them by.

My desire is to communicate to others how the Lord led me to healing and wholeness. Then they, too, can experience a life free from anxiety and panic.

Chapter One

"The Thing Which I Greatly Feared Is Come Upon Me"
Job 3:25

It was a steamy, 95-degree August Friday. The kind of day that when you step outdoors, you perspire instantly. And this was my wedding day. Imagine the thoughts of a young bride picturing herself walking down the aisle with wilted flowers and droopy hair. Well, that's the way it was for me in 1988.

My husband and I had planned the wedding in just two short weeks. Not because we had to get married, but because we thought it made sense. And I suppose to our 20- and 23-year-old minds it did. We were finishing our education and grew tired of the college roommate scene. Living together was out of the question for us due to our beliefs. Plus, we had already been engaged for more than a year. Our families had vastly different views of what a wedding celebration should be. So -- what better idea than to throw together a small "immediate relatives only" wedding. Right?

My mother and father had tried to persuade me to move back home until graduation, instead of rushing into a marriage. They also wanted us to get married in a church rather than by a public official or a judge at city hall. But we had checked around, and every church we contacted required pre-marital counseling -- some classes lasted up to six or eight months! Finally, we found one that would marry us after just one meeting with the pastor. So

1

that's the church we went with.

The wedding went smoothly, and we had a small reception for the 12 guests back at my parents' home. After cake and punch, Jeff and I hopped into my little Volkswagen Rabbit, which we had purchased four days earlier, to head out to the honeymoon suite at a local hotel. But the car wouldn't start. We tried everything to get it going but ended up taking his parents' car. We would deal with the Rabbit the next day.

Saturday turned out to be a 95-degree day as well. We had the automobile towed to the used car dealer where we had purchased it, and they gave us a loaner to drive while the starter was being replaced. Because it was already late in the morning, we decided not to go away for the weekend but to just do some shopping and relax until our car was ready. To our dismay, when we came out of the store where we had been shopping, the loaner car wouldn't start! We had to call the dealer again, and they picked us up in a tow truck and took us back to the lot. By the time we got another loaner and pulled away, I felt as if I had spent my entire first day of marriage with a used car salesman!

Well, that weekend seemed to be the triggering factor in my experience with panic attacks. I had failed to see that I was headed straight for a brick wall at about 200 miles per hour. But when you're 20 you're invincible -- right? At the age of 20, within a one-month time period, I found myself in a new apartment, in a new town, with a new husband, with new responsibilities, starting a new job and facing my senior year of college. All that combined was enough for a score of 161 on the Social Readjustment Rating Scale -- the one that indicates how likely you are to suffer from a serious illness if too many events occur within a one-year period. But I was invincible. I could handle it.

Two days later, I found myself standing over the bathroom sink trying to brush my teeth. I say "trying" because a strange sensation came over me. My heart pounded, my hands trembled and

I was light-headed. I sat down to relax for a minute, expecting this strange sensation to pass. But I felt as if I were in a fog -- as though I had to concentrate extremely hard to fight this "cloudy feeling." As if I wasn't really there.

After about a half hour or so, I left the house and went about my day at college and work at a local pharmacy. I attributed the episode to the fact that I was taking a heavy-duty antibiotic for an infection, and I had always been sensitive to strong medication.

A few days later, while I was working at the pharmacy checkout, it happened again. Those strange sensations slowly creeped up on me. My heart pounded, my hands trembled, and I had to concentrate very hard to talk to the customers on whom I was waiting. It was similar to the feeling most people have when waking up from general anesthesia. You want to be alert, but just can't quite bring yourself to that point. You feel as if you are merely observing what is going on around you without actually being part of it.

When I went into the back room to sit down, my boss said I was probably reacting to stress. He mentioned that I might be having a panic or anxiety attack. Immediately, my defenses went up. I thought that I absolutely could not be having a panic attack. In fact, that was the last thing I wanted to hear.

I knew all I wanted to know about anxiety and panic attacks. My father had suffered from them for the past year and a half and had been in and out of the stress management unit of a local hospital two or three times. He had become a different person. It was so hard to visit Dad or take him back to the hospital after he'd had an eight-hour leave pass. How could he belong there? The other patients really needed the help -- one girl was anorexic, a few others had severe depression -- but Dad? Surely the doctor had made a mistake! I remember being afraid I would somehow "catch" what was going around up in that stress management unit.

Before the panic attacks, my father had always been a

strong-minded, opinionated, hard-working Christian man. Now he was crippled by fear and struggling to keep his job. And I was the daughter who had been told all her life that she was ''just like her father.'' Well, here was one area in which this eldest daughter was bound and determined not to be like her father!

Like many people who suffer or have suffered from anxiety and panic attacks, I searched desperately for a medical physical reason for my symptoms. I went to general practitioners who said I had everything from gastroenteritis to a viral infection. I had every major blood test and every test showed there was nothing physically wrong. So then why was I having such strange symptoms -- heart palpitations, nausea, vomiting, diarrhea, fatigue and that awful ''cloudy, floaty'' feeling?

One doctor tried to put me on Vistril and then finally Buspar for my ''nerves.'' But to no avail. I continued to suffer and even went from 128 to 103 pounds in a matter of weeks.

One afternoon, after I had been suffering with the symptoms for about three months, my husband, Jeff, and I went to a local shopping mall. I hadn't been feeling well, and we were trying to get my mind off it. I remember running into a former junior high school teacher and having to concentrate extremely hard to carry on a conversation. The symptoms were coming back. I was in a ''familiar'' place with a ''safe'' person, but they came anyway. So we walked on and Jeff purchased a beautiful sweater for me, hoping it would make me feel better. Well, we had put it on a new credit card, and I remember being upset because now in addition to our usual credit card payment, we'd have to make a payment on the new charge card. More anxiety!

The symptoms kept building, and on the way home I felt very nervous and high strung. Not only did I feel like I wasn't really there and as though I were in a cloud or a fog, but I was also having tingling sensations in my hands and feet and my brain felt ''staticky and fuzzy.'' I could only imagine what my new husband was thinking when I told him this!

When we arrived home, Jeff decided he was going to look at new cars (more anxiety!) on his way to classes at the police academy. He asked if I would be all right, and I assured him there was nothing he could do for me. By that time my symptoms had grown into a full-blown panic attack. My brain literally felt like it was flying apart inside my head. I called my mother and she insisted I call my father's psychiatrist, which until then I had refused to do. But I felt so awful and desperate that I finally picked up the phone and called Dr. Rajdev Grewal (pronounced gray-wall).

Dr. Grewal talked to me over the phone, and by my state of mind and description of my symptoms, she knew I was having a panic attack. She made an appointment for me for the next day and instructed my mother to come over with some of my father's medication. I took a one milligram tablet of Xanax and was asleep within 20 minutes.

When I awoke, I was exhausted. Panic attacks do that to you. My mother was still there with me doing the dishes and cleaning up the small apartment in which Jeff and I lived. I had reached the point where even the littlest things overwhelmed me. Mom said she would go with me to the doctor the next day. I felt like I was giving in -- it had won! The thing which I greatly feared had come upon me -- I was having anxiety and panic attacks and would seek a psychiatrist's treatment. What was in store for me next?

Chapter Two

"No One Understands"
  Romans 3:11 (AMP)

That night I slept soundly. The day's events had worn me out, and I couldn't wait to go to the doctor the next morning to get the relief and help I needed. There was one thing that bothered me: I could not be honest with Jeff about seeing my father's doctor. Jeff was convinced that Dr. Grewal had turned Dad into the frightened man he was. Nonetheless, I knew this woman doctor could give me the help I desperately needed. My mother drove me to Dr. Grewal's office, which was about 40 minutes away. During the one-hour session, the doctor asked a lot of questions -- about my health, my personality, my education, activities, husband and family. She had treated four other members of my dad's family for anxiety or depression, so she knew something about our medical history.

After our discussion, Dr. Grewal concluded I was indeed suffering from panic disorder. It was a diagnosis I didn't really want to hear, but I was ready to accept it because I wanted so desperately to feel better.

The doctor told me that the combination of a genetic predisposition toward anxiety and depression and a stressful environment brought on the panic attacks. When I thought about it, I realized I had let myself get worn out physically and emotionally. I had been doing whatever it took to maintain a high grade point average for the past three years of college. Plus, I was working, and I was in a relationship that really wasn't good for me.

I was given prescriptions for Xanax and Norpramin, antianxiety and anti-depressant medications. I also made an appointment for the following week. In addition, Dr. Grewal told me I needed to either take the semester off from school or quit my job at the pharmacy to get on the road to recovery.

Of course, I didn't see how I could quit either one. I needed to stay in college to keep my scholarship, and I needed to work because my husband didn't make enough money to cover our living expenses. I also didn't think I could make it through an entire week until my next appointment. But the doctor assured me that I could call her if I had any trouble. With that, I left and my mother drove me home.

There were so many questions going through my head: Why was this happening to me? I was a good Christian and had been since I had given my life to the Lord a few years earlier. Didn't God care about me anymore? Was this my punishment for marrying a non-Christian? What would I do now -- about work, school, my husband? What would his family think? What would my friends think?

When Jeff got home late that evening from working at the local grocery store and attending the police academy, I told him the doctor's diagnosis: panic disorder. His response was one of disbelief -- how does a 21-year-old get panic disorder? There was nothing wrong with me, he said, it was all in my head. Besides, he didn't want a "psycho" for a wife. Of course, when he asked if I saw Dr. Grewal, I said "no" to prevent further hostility. Instead, I told him I saw another doctor in the same building.

Jeff was not thrilled that I was taking medication, either. He said I didn't need it and if I was "strong enough mentally" I could overcome this without drugs. I knew how I felt, though, and I knew that he just didn't understand -- nor did he want to try.

You can imagine Jeff's reaction when I told him the last

7

tidbit of information: that I needed to quit work or quit school. He immediately blew up and said we couldn't afford for me to quit either. After a few words and a few tears on my part, we agreed I would quit working at the pharmacy. We decided I would take additional student loan dollars available to me from a local foundation to help us financially.

I felt so defeated. I had always been an overachiever and very active -- your classic "Type A" personality. To realize I would have to quit my job and just do the bare minimum to get by in school was a major upset. But my body was clearly sending out signals, and I had no choice but to take care of myself.

People with panic disorder are notoriously concerned about what other people think. My immediate family was supportive and helpful after having just been through similar circumstances with my father. Jeff's family, however, had never dealt with someone who had a mental or emotional illness. They had just as much difficulty understanding my situation as Jeff did. In their family, everyone was "tough" or "strong-minded." They couldn't understand how a 21-year-old could be under so much stress that it caused a "mental breakdown." It really didn't do any good to explain to them that this was an illness I had to deal with, just like some people deal with ulcers, diabetes or cancer.

As for my friends, I didn't discuss my condition with them much, either. They knew I was sick because of my weight loss and constant trouble with nausea or diarrhea -- I rarely went anywhere without Coke, soda crackers and Kaopectate! But they had no idea how I was suffering. I remember some well-meaning individuals saying that I needed to "just pick myself up by the bootstraps and get over it." But in this situation that is the furthest thing from possible. You don't just "snap out of it." I felt everyone around me, with the exception of my immediate family, was thinking, "Wow, she really lost it. That's too bad because she had so much going for her."

What no one realized was that I wanted more than anything to just "snap out of it" and feel like my old, normal, happy, energetic self again. I didn't want to let my family, friends, employers and college professors down. What was happening to me was all too common for people suffering from anxiety and panic attacks. Friends and family do not understand and therefore can't give the loving support and encouragement that are so desperately needed. Often, as it was in my case, because those in the sufferer's circle of influence don't understand, they continue to expect the individual to perform at his or her usual high levels. And when the sufferer has to say "no" or cut back on some activities, it can lead to isolation and rejection. This further aggravates the condition.

I was very fortunate, however, to have someone who could relate to me -- my father. He had been where I was and had progressed enough with his recovery to offer support. At times, he literally had to convince me that I would be all right if I ventured out of my apartment to go to school or to the grocery store. Perhaps one of the greatest benefits was when I would describe a symptom and he could say, "Yes, I've experienced that before." This was so much better than the usual reaction when I'd try to describe something to others -- they just looked at me like I was crazy when I wanted so much for them to say, "Yes, I know what you mean."

During that period, with extra time on my hands, I was able to get my focus back on God. I began to pray more than ever and listen to Christian tapes and Christian radio. I watched Christian television and read the Bible and any Christian self-help books and materials I could get my hands on. I was clinging to God like never before. I thoroughly believe that some days He literally carried me through with His strength. On my own, I'd have never made it.

Shortly after I began praying, Jeff accepted a new job making about $250 more per month. He would have excellent benefits and the opportunity for overtime. And his boss was a

Christian! I was amazed that God cared so much about me.

It was at about that point as well that I realized I had indeed been out of fellowship with God for the past few years. I hadn't been attending church or praying regularly and thus hadn't been feeding my spirit. I had enough good teaching in my life to know that if you don't make any ''deposits,'' when you go to ''withdraw'' there won't be anything to take out. And so it was with me spiritually -- my well had gone dry and when I went to draw water out, there was nothing.

I'm not saying that if I had been going to church and praying, I wouldn't have ended up suffering from panic attacks. However, I began to realize that I needed help from both doctors and the Lord to overcome this disorder and enjoy life again.

Chapter Three

"In The World You Have Tribulation And Trials"
John 16:33 (AMP)

The Learning Stage

One thing I learned quickly was that I couldn't possibly overcome a disorder without first gathering all the information about it that I could. In other words, I had to know what I was dealing with in order to know what my next step should be.

So off I went to the library and bookstores to bring home everything about anxiety and panic attacks that I could get my hands on. Unfortunately, there weren't very many. But I checked out two books, purchased another and jumped right into them.

I was relieved to know there was actually a medical definition for the symptoms and disorder from which I was suffering. Webster's New World Dictionary defines panic as "a sudden, unreasoning, hysterical fear." The American Psychiatric Association, in its pamphlet on Panic Disorder, says that in order for a panic attack to be classed as part of a panic disorder, it must be one of four such anxious episodes in a four-week period and must include at least four of the following symptoms:
· Sweating
· Shortness of breath
· Heart palpitations
· Chest discomfort
· Unsteady feelings

· Choking or smothering sensations
· Tingling
· Hot or cold flashes
· Faintness
· Trembling
· Nausea or abdominal distress
· Feelings of unreality
· Fears of losing control, dying or going insane

It's important to note that not all attacks or all people have the same symptoms.

The name panic attack was given to such an episode because of the urgent need to get out and run to someplace safe. After reading this information, I agreed with my doctor's diagnosis. It was also somewhat comforting to read the many accounts of people who had suffered just like me. They were dealing with the same "enemy," and their lives were hindered in much the same way.

Almost everyone at some point in their lives experiences anxiety. Maybe stress on the job or at home, or both, leads to a heightened or "sensitized" state of anxiety. However, this is not the type of generalized anxiety that a person with panic disorder faces. Unlike a person who can trace stress to work or family problems, the panic disorder sufferer has nervous symptoms for no apparent reason. But why? What caused the disorder in this person and not the next?

Research into the causes of panic disorder has been on the rise in recent years. According to surveys, more women than men, by a ratio of two to one, suffer from panic disorder, which knows no racial, economic or geographic boundaries. Because sufferers many times hide their illness, and medical practitioners not familiar with the disorder often misdiagnose it, it's difficult to determine just how widespread panic disorder is. In a recent study of the general population by the National Institute of Mental Health, however, 10 percent of those interviewed reported having spontaneous panic attacks. The best recent estimate places the number of Americans suffering from panic disorder at 1.5 percent, or more than three million people. These people regularly suffer from the panic attack -- the crisis phase of the disorder.

Recent studies have also shown that panic disorder's roots are indeed physical as well as psychological. Panic disorder runs in families, which supports the theory that it is inherited. In people with panic disorder, there is a problem with a neurotransmitter, norepinephrine, being released in too large of quantities. Neurotransmitters are part of the brain's intricate chemical system that communicates with the rest of the human body.

Not only does a genetic predisposition toward panic disorder play an important role in whether a person will develop the condition, but the environment does also. It is important to look at how one's parents handled stress. Did they constantly worry? Was the family dysfunctional? Were abuse or neglect prevalent? Such factors, coupled with a family history of depression or anxiety, can give a person a tendency toward the illness. Because the disorder typically begins when victims are in their 20's, the environment at that time plays a key role, as well.

In my family, my mother seemed to have mastered stress. Nothing ever appeared to bother her. If it did, she was able to roll with the punches. She had a lot of practice, though, going through alcoholism with my father in the '70s and then, of course, his more recent challenge with panic attacks. Dad, on the other hand, would get preoccupied with something and obsess about it until it was resolved. My younger sister, Dana, and I were not abused or neglected, although the family did have a time of financial crisis when the real estate market plunged in the early '80s. However, I don't believe my environment during childhood played a significant role in the onset of panic disorder.

I was one of those kids that was always on the go. My

mother reminded me that when I was 11, my pediatrician had to explain to me that when I added something to my schedule, I needed to eliminate something else. Instead of playing on one ball team in the summer, I played on two, and was also involved in cheerleading, debate, basketball, cross country and just about every other activity available to a junior high and high schooler. My parents tried their best to limit my activities. But even back then I was headstrong and wound up with mononucleosis. I wish I'd have learned to slow down!

After studying the disorder and reflecting back to my childhood, I was still amazed to discover that the feelings I experienced during a panic attack were actually normal. My body was initiating a reaction to danger. But what danger? Who or what told my body that I was in danger? What a surprise to find out that in effect, I had told my body I was in danger! I had triggered my brain to put into action the adrenaline, or "fight or flight," response.

This fight or flight response is nature's built-in way of protecting us from external dangers. For instance, if you hear a noise in the middle of the night, your immediate response is to become aroused to protect yourself and your family. The body releases adrenaline, norepinephrine and other hormones that constrict the blood vessels in the body's extremities. This allows more blood to flow to the brain and larger muscles for added strength. Your heart pounds, digestion shuts down, breathing becomes more rapid and your muscles tense up. Now you are ready to defend yourself and your family or run away as fast as you can.

But when there is no imminent danger and your body still reacts this way, the accompanying feelings are very uncomfortable. You can set this response into motion by getting all worked up with worry, fear or fret -- whether it be consciously or subconsciously. It is generated by the mind through internal anxiety and fear, rather than external danger.

My pastor, Dr. C. Herschel Gammill of The Cathedral of

Life in Canton, Ohio, has been known to define this type of fear as False Expectations Appearing Real. In other words, we are afraid and get ourselves all worked up over some form of danger that is not even real.

This closely ties in with what is called anticipatory anxiety. This is the fear and accompanying symptoms that panic disorder sufferers feel when they first think about doing something. Lucinda Bassett, in her book *From Panic to Power*, calls it the "what-if" syndrome.

Anticipatory anxiety, for me, was paralyzing. I would literally "what-if" myself into anxious symptoms thinking and worrying about an event that was to happen in days, weeks or even months: "What if I have to cancel?" "What will they think?" "What if I'm nauseous or have diarrhea?" "What if I get those spacey, floaty feelings?" "What if I have a full-blown panic attack?" "What if I need to leave?"

My doctor would often ask me, "What would be the worst thing that could happen?" This would help me straighten out my perspective. When I could look at it clearly, the worst thing that could happen was never as bad as the thoughts and following symptoms I allowed myself to have. The anticipation was most often much worse than the actual event. Sometimes our minds can be so creative!

Once I learned to keep myself from creating a fiasco before it happened, I was able to "practice" doing more things. The more I was able to accomplish something and come back saying "that wasn't so bad," the more confidence I gained and the less time I spent dealing with anticipatory anxiety. Sometimes you just have to say, "So what if...!"

I also learned about some of the other common associations with the disorder. For instance, most sufferers tend to stay away from situations or places where episodes have occurred. They may stop riding elevators or going to restaurants if these activities seem

15

to trigger the attacks. This is called avoidance and can lead to the sufferer becoming reclusive. The person may feel it is better to suffer alone than to risk enduring the attacks in public, because there's no telling when the next one might occur. But the attacks keep happening.

I am grateful that my father didn't let me become too reclusive. His encouraging me to go out and continue my normal activities, even though I had symptoms, kept me from hiding from the fear. Even Jeff, although his manner could have been more sympathetic and caring, helped tremendously because he wouldn't allow me to become a prisoner in my own home. We still visited his family regularly and went out to dinner or engaged in some other activity that challenged me to face the fear no matter how uncomfortable I was.

I believe that because of Dad and Jeff, my problems with agoraphobia, which often accompanies panic disorder, were kept to a minimum. Agoraphobia literally means "fear of the marketplace." Strangely enough, not only are people who suffer from panic disorder afraid of being around too many people and having an episode, but they are also afraid of being alone. So they create a "safe place," usually home, and "safe people," usually family or close friends, and thus their lifestyles become confined.

Getting the Medical Help You Need

Medical help is essential for people with panic disorder. If left untreated, the disorder can even more severely disrupt the victim's life, making work, family activities and even day-to-day living next to impossible.

Panic disorder is often difficult to diagnose because it mimics other medical or psychiatric problems. For instance, a medical doctor may diagnose a patient with heart disease, thyroid problems, respiratory problems or hypoglycemia when in reality he or she is suffering from panic disorder. It is not uncommon for victims to go from doctor to doctor looking for help, only to give up and doubt their own mental stability.

That's when a psychiatrist who is trained in correctly diagnosing panic disorder and other psychiatric or emotional illnesses can help. After establishing that the patient doesn't have any other physical illness that could be causing the panic symptoms, the psychiatrist begins to assemble a complete medical history.

Once panic disorder is diagnosed, the psychiatrist will most likely begin to employ any of a number of medications available to help ease the patient's symptoms so he or she can begin to learn about the condition. (We'll deal with the topic of medication in more detail in Chapter Four.)

Dr. Massood R. Babai, chairman of the Department of Psychiatry at Summa/St. Thomas Hospital in Akron, Ohio, says that once a patient responds well to a medication and the symptoms are less threatening, the best way to treat the disorder is to use a combination of cognitive and behavioral therapy.

Cognitive therapy includes educating the patient about his or her condition and the agoraphobia, anticipatory anxiety or other coexisting problems. Gaining knowledge helps to restructure the way the patient thinks about the disorder.

Behavioral therapy includes working on the sufferer's actions and having him or her perform certain activities or go to certain places in spite of the symptoms. The psychiatrist works with the patient, teaching him or her to employ relaxation techniques and breathing exercises. Then, the sufferer gradually enters situations or places he or she may have been avoiding. For example, a person will go to a shopping mall or a restaurant where he has experienced problems in the past. He may not purchase or eat anything during this venture, but it is a victory to just be there and window shop or have a glass of ice water at a table. It is important to expect to have symptoms -- but to concentrate on other things to take attention away from these symptoms. With each venture, it becomes easier to go to these places, and the sufferer's confidence grows.

Combining medication, cognitive and behavioral therapy has helped nine out of 10 sufferers recover and return to normal life activities. Diagnosing panic disorder in its early stages has also recently begun to reduce complications, while research and new medical education are helping more and more patients get the treatment they need.

Dealing with Stress

As the title of this chapter indicates, Jesus Christ Himself said, "In the world you have tribulation and trials." There's no getting around the stresses of day-to-day living on this earth. However -- there are quite a few things we can do about stress. The first is to learn as much as we can about it.

First, there are two types of stress: *distress* and *eustress*. Distress has a negative connotation. It is the type of stress that you perceive to be the cause of anxiety. For instance, family conflicts or work problems would be considered distress. Typically, you brace yourself against this type of stress. Your perception of the "stressor" as an extreme danger triggers a fight or flight response. Robert Handly, in his book *Anxiety and Panic Attacks, Their Cause and Cure*, says distress has a cumulative effect on the body and can make one subject to panic attacks.

Eustress, however, is viewed more positively and is not seen as an extreme danger. For instance, a vacation, holiday, birth of a baby, marriage, promotion or other positive life event is a stressor. But because of our attitude toward it, we don't initiate the fight or flight response in reaction to it. Instead, we can deal with it and let it go -- and thus it does not have a cumulative effect on the body. However, panic disorder sufferers often turn eustress into distress. Vacations, Christmas and other positive life events can become traumatic instead of joyful because of "what-if-ing" and anticipatory anxiety.

Once again referring to Robert Handly, your attitude toward life's events determines whether you will have distress or eustress. It is possible to reshape the way you think and react to turn distress into eustress.

If you have a high number of stressors in your life that complicate your condition of panic disorder, you may need to eliminate any sources of stress that you can. For example, you'll recall I had to either quit my job or quit school so I could focus on my recovery. You may need to cut back on a certain number of activities or commitments, eliminate the extra part-time job, or stop babysitting the neighbors' children. These decisions may not be popular among family or friends, but you need to think about your health.

As for stressors that cannot be eliminated, it is important to adopt a new attitude toward them. Do only what absolutely needs to be done and nothing more. Try to live in the moment and enjoy what you are doing -- don't get yourself all worked up during one task because you are thinking ahead to the next 14 things you still need to get done. Prioritize your activities so you get the most important things done first. If you get to the next ones, fine. If not, they are probably not so earth-shattering that they can't wait until the next day.

You may be thinking, "I want to enjoy life. I want to keep myself from getting all worked up and have a more relaxed attitude -- but how? That's my problem!"

Everyone reading this book probably knows someone who is so laid-back that almost nothing seems to bother them. A bomb could go off beside these people and they'd say, "Gee, that was awfully loud." But those of us with anxiety or panic would immediately jump up, our heart would pound and we'd try to figure out what happened.

One of my favorite preachers of the Gospel, Joyce Meyer of Life in the Word Ministries in Fenton, Missouri, has often told

19

about the "old Joyce" -- before the Lord taught her to be a calm, cool and collected Christian. Joyce used to be very easily excited -- especially when her kids were young and they were sitting down at the dinner table. Inevitably, one of her kids would spill some milk, and that would set her off. She'd rant and rave about how hard she'd worked to prepare dinner and how she didn't have time to be cleaning up after them, etc., etc. Well, the milk would run all over and get into the cracks and flow down the table legs. It was during one of these episodes, Joyce relates, that "The Holy Spirit came unto me saying: 'Joyce, no matter how much you scream and holler and rant and rave, and no matter how big a fuss you make, all the screaming in the world is not going to make that milk go back up those table legs and into the glass.'"

Hearing Joyce tell this story had a great impact on me. You know, you can hear something over and over and hear it and hear it. But then one day, you finally HEAR it and it gets into your spirit. It was as if God was saying to me through Joyce not to let myself get all bent out of shape about something I could not control.

It takes practice to learn to be relaxed and take life as it comes. The relaxation techniques and coping strategies I will discuss in later chapters will help tremendously with this effort. But perhaps the biggest benefit is to learn to decipher what we can and cannot control.

I have already mentioned how important it is to learn to identify and eliminate those stressors that can be eliminated and to prioritize the rest of your activities. Stressors that cannot be eliminated, especially those that pop up unexpectedly, need to be evaluated. You need to ask yourself, "What can I do about this particular situation?" If there is a definite action that can be taken to address or better the situation, by all means, do so. If the situation is beyond your realm of control or ability to address, then you must realize so and let it go. You need to practice this evaluation process to get better and better at it. I'll try to give you some specific examples.

Example 1: Your car breaks down and needs repairs, so you are without a vehicle one evening after work...the evening you were to drive your children and the neighbor's children to ball practice. When you feel yourself getting all tense and excited about this, ask yourself, "What can I do about this particular situation?" Clearly, you cannot make the mechanic work any faster. So, you are going to have to call the neighbor and ask him to drive one more time because your car is in the shop. If he cannot do so, then the kids will just have to miss practice. Call their coach and explain the problem. Then don't give the situation any more thought. There was nothing more in your power that could be done. You asked the neighbor to take your turn, but he couldn't. Did he waste any time saying "no" to you? Probably not. Then don't fret about something over which you had no control.

Example 2: You were planning to get the lawn mowed and trimmed this evening before it rains because your yard is starting to look like a hay field. But the storm front moved in quicker than expected, and you aren't going to be able to get to it. Again, when you feel the tension and stress rising, step back and ask yourself, "What can I do about this particular situation?" You cannot control the weather, but you can control how you react to it. It is not a life or death situation -- if your grass is the longest in the neighborhood for a week, who will it hurt? There are probably many other chores you can do since this one is off the "to-do list" for tonight. Decide to do one of the other chores instead and get to the grass in a few days when you have the time and the weather permits.

Once you practice these evaluations a few times, it will be easier and easier to react calmly to situations beyond your control. You may even find yourself becoming more like that person I mentioned earlier -- the one who never lets anything bother him or

21

her. In the process of getting there, though, it may be helpful to channel the stress adrenaline to another activity when you feel it rising. Since your car is in the repair shop, go jogging. Or since it is raining, do some vacuuming or an aerobics video. You've got to eliminate that energy somehow.

And if you are really having a tough time with evaluating a situation and letting go, give yourself a set time for thinking about that or any other problems. Write on a piece of paper anything that has caused you stress that day. Then allow yourself 15 minutes to think about and evaluate those things further. When this 15-minute period is up, so is the thinking and evaluating. If the subject creeps into your thoughts at other times throughout the day, remind yourself that you will concern yourself with that circumstance at the allotted time.

The bottom line is that we choose to either get worked up over something (react in the flesh) or to behave peacefully and calmly -- the way Jesus would have us react (react in the Spirit). In Romans 8, we learn about the mind of the flesh and the mind of the Spirit. The mind of the flesh is death, the Bible says, but the mind of the Spirit is life and peace. There is a constant war between the flesh and the Spirit. But each time we choose to cast a vote for the Spirit, we are pleasing Jesus Christ, who is there to see us through each struggle.

The latter portion of this chapter reminds me of the eagle in one of my favorite scriptures. You know, the eagle just soars on the wind currents and doesn't work hard at flying through the air. You never see an eagle frantically flapping his wings and wearing himself out trying to fly. Instead, he spreads his wings and flows with the currents. We need to do the same thing in our lives -- just go with the flow and stop wearing ourselves out while fighting to be in control. Because, ultimately, if Jesus Christ is our Lord and Savior, He is in control anyway.

But they that wait upon the Lord shall renew their strength; They shall mount up with wings as eagles; They shall run, and not be weary; And they shall walk, and not faint.   *Isaiah 40:31*

Chapter Four

"I Can Do All Things Through Christ Which Strengtheneth Me"   *Philippians 4:13*

Probably the last thing a Christian suffering from anxiety and panic attacks wants to hear is that anxiety is a sin. But the truth is, it is! The Bible clearly tells us in Philippians 4:6, "Do not fret or have any anxiety about anything, but in every circumstance and in everything, by prayer and petition, with thanksgiving, continue to make your wants known to God" (AMP). If we do this, we are promised in verse seven that "God's peace which transcends all understanding shall garrison and mount guard over your hearts and minds in Christ Jesus."

In Matthew 6:25, Jesus tells us not to worry about tomorrow, wondering what we will eat or drink or wear. He further says that God takes care of the birds and lilies and that we are much more important than the birds and flowers -- we are His children! He says our Heavenly Father knows what we need and if we simply put Him first, all these things shall be added unto us.

Sounds simple, right? Maybe it's not so simple. But it is possible! The Lord would not instruct us to do something if it were out of our realm of capability. The truth is that when we are worried or anxious, we have taken our focus off the Father, who is the solution, and put it on the problem or circumstance. And when we do this, we are really having more faith in the problem than we have in the Lord. We're not trusting God enough to take care of us and our circumstances. We need to tell our problem how big our God is rather than tell our God how big our problem is.

Please don't misunderstand me -- people who have panic disorder can't just turn off worry and anxiety like a light switch and simply say, "I'm not going to do that anymore." And I didn't bring up the sin issue to bring condemnation on sufferers. We just need to be aware that it is a sin to worry and be anxious. We must have as a goal not to make a practice of worry and anxiety and to do our part to be free from it...which is probably why you are reading this book. So you are on the right track.

In this chapter I will outline the steps I put into action to overcome my ordeal with panic disorder. But first, I'd like to discuss some of the most common symptoms of panic, as well as some of the most effective coping strategies.

Common Symptoms and How to Cope

Every person suffering from panic disorder has his or her own set of symptoms. For one person, the most common discomfort might be chest pains similar to those of a heart attack. For another, it might be nausea, vomiting and dizziness. In either case, the discomfort to each person is equally severe and must be dealt with.

1) Heart Racing and/or Palpitations -- Just prior to an attack or during the actual panic attack itself, a sufferer may notice his or her heart racing or experience an irregular beating pattern. Obviously, the sufferer needs to be sure there are no heart conditions present and should consult a physician to rule this out. But once it has been established that the racing or palpitations are associated with panic disorder, the less attention given to this wildly pumping organ, the better. It may cause discomfort and concern, but believe it or not, the heart can pump very fast without causing physical trouble or damage. Although you may think your heart will leap right out of your chest, rest assured that it won't and that your body will work to regulate itself back to its normal heart rhythm. It may happen over a period of hours, but it will happen -- and your body will function normally again.

Whatever you do, don't be alarmed. This will only make for a longer period of fast or irregular beats. Simply tell yourself that no one around you can tell that your heart is racing. Also emphasize to yourself that your heart beating this way will not hurt you and that it will return to normal. Then, try to get your mind off it by becoming engrossed in another activity.

2) Chest Pains -- Closely related to heart racing and palpitations is the fear of having a heart attack. Many sufferers of panic disorder display the symptoms of a heart attack in the form of severe tightness and constriction in the chest area. These sufferers often end up in the emergency room at a local hospital several times before this particular symptom is attributed to anxiety or panic. Once again, after you rule out any heart problems, the next step is to learn to cope effectively with the pain. When the discomfort first arrives, tell yourself that it is simply a by-product of anxiety and that it will not harm you. Trying to get your mind off the pain to keep it from escalating may work if it is done at the pain's early onset. However, this may not be effective if you are already in a lot of pain. If a distraction is impossible, you may need to lie down and practice relaxation techniques (detailed later in this chapter) until the muscles in that area loosen. Nonetheless, hard as it may seem, the less attention you give the discomfort, the less you will have to endure it.

Some people find the chest pains so severe that they need pain relief medication. Your physician may be able to prescribe something for your use during episodes that are too painful to handle without medicinal relief.

3) Choking Sensations -- These symptoms are characterized by a tightness or constriction in the throat. The sufferer may feel that he or she is unable to breathe or swallow -- believing that the esophagus and windpipe have done everything but close. These particular feelings may cause a person to avoid going out to eat in a public place or with a group for fear of choking in front of others.

If this symptom occurs often, keep a glass of water or other beverage close by to sip when a flare-up happens. Taking deep breaths, changing your position or activity, or possibly even trying to eat something like a popsicle can help, too. But do know that you will not suffocate or choke, and tell yourself no harm will be done. Getting involved in an activity to get your mind off what you are feeling may also be a good idea.

4) Nausea and Vomiting -- Stomach upset is commonly associated with people who suffer from anxiety and panic attacks. Unfortunately, a fear of vomiting in public can keep sufferers from going many places and add to their seclusion. However, in the nine years that I have dealt with the disorder and nausea, one of my most prominent symptoms, I have never vomited in public. I always managed to get to a restroom or other place where I could handle the upset in private.

The nausea and vomiting I dealt with were so profuse and at times so unexpected that it was almost debilitating. I can remember feeling fine one minute, and the next minute a strong wave of nausea would come over me. I would have to run from whatever I was doing to get some fresh air and try to prevent the vomiting. It was helpful to have soda crackers and pretzels in my purse to keep something on my stomach at all times. I also relied heavily on Coca Cola to settle it. In addition, my doctor prescribed Phenergan pills for me to use as needed when the symptoms were particularly severe. One side effect of this medication, however, is drowsiness, so I had to take that into consideration before using the pills.

5) Diarrhea -- Gastrointestinal ills are very common physical symptoms associated with anxiety and panic disorder. And diarrhea is perhaps one of the most annoying. I've heard people give accounts of their battles with spastic colon and irritable bowel

27

syndrome that seem quite humorous. But, as in my case, there is never any humor the moment you are going through it. In fact, the episodes themselves can be quite painful.

Relief can be found, however, in various ways. Over-the-counter remedies such as Kaopectate and Imodium AD have proven quite effective for me. Better yet was a prescription anti-diarrheal called dycyclomine, which can also be taken at the onset of an attack. This medication helped greatly with the pain and cramping associated with each episode. Of course, before taking any medicine, seek a doctor's advice.

With gastrointestinal upset, you may feel as if you don't have the freedom to eat the foods you want, when you want to eat them. For example, if you have an important business dinner to attend or plan to go out for a special evening, you don't want to be plagued with diarrhea. Avoiding fried and spicy foods during these events can help to ward off an episode. You may be watering at the mouth for that deep fried shrimp, but it's better to go with broiled or baked chicken and a bland side dish instead.

6) Hot Flashes and Blushing -- There's blushing and then there's BLUSHING! Many young people blush when they are introduced to a good-looking member of the opposite sex. That's normal. But some people, including me, turn beet red at the slightest thing during the most inopportune times. My face gets deep red sometimes, and the color runs right down my neck. People have asked me if I feel okay, or even if I have a sunburn, to which my face promptly responds with an even more intense color.

I'll admit, this problem was quite perplexing and even embarrassing. I remember avoiding certain situations and people for fear of blushing. However, after I learned a little more about it, it didn't bother me as much.

In her book, *Peace From Nervous Suffering,* Dr. Claire Weekes explains that blushing is caused when the nerves that control the blood vessels in the face and neck become startled by emotion. These nerves and blood vessels suddenly release their grip, allowing blood to flood the vessels. Trying not to blush means tensely concentrating on one's face. And the more attention nerves get, the more easily startled they become. So, of course, the more likely they are to lose their grip and bring a blush.

Once I realized what caused the blushing, I finally learned to allow myself to blush no matter what. It was difficult, but soon I didn't really care whether my face turned red or not. And the less I cared, the less red I became. I also realized, after looking in the mirror, that the warm sensation I felt was often worse than the actual color of my face. Many times, the blushing wasn't as noticeable as I thought.

7) Sleeping Problems -- Often sufferers of panic disorder have trouble falling asleep. This can be quite frustrating, since dealing with symptoms or even a full-blown panic attack during the day can be exhausting. And if you have to go to work the next morning, lying awake looking at the clock for a good part of the night is not what you want to do.

I remember on many occasions thinking, "How am I going to be able to work tomorrow if I don't get to sleep?"

When sleep problems plagued me, my doctor told me that as long as I could get four or so hours of sleep, my body would be fine. She also assured me that when my body was tired, it would sleep, and I could try catching a short nap during the day or early evening if possible.

The following activities might help you in falling asleep: get some form of daily exercise (but don't work out too close to bedtime), avoid caffeine in the afternoon and evening, and stay away from television shows or movies that are too disturbing or stimulating. Drinking a glass of warm milk has a calming, drowsy effect, as does reading a good book. Perhaps you could incorporate scripture reading or prayer and meditation as part of your bedtime routine. Ending each day with the Lord always makes good sense!

29

8) Fear of Going Crazy -- Many fears plague a person suffering from panic disorder. And most have something to do with the thought of losing control because panic disorder sufferers are usually known for being "control freaks." The last thing a sufferer wants to lose control of is his or her mind. So naturally, a fear of going crazy would play a major role in the sufferer's thoughts.

During a full-blown panic attack, you may have the feeling that your brain is "flying apart," and because you cannot control the sensation you may indeed think you are going crazy. However, you should simply let the panic attack run its course, and when it dies down you will begin to feel more like yourself again.

A statement that my doctor made brought me much comfort and assurance during these times:

"People who are concerned about going crazy are not the ones who go crazy. It is those people who don't realize they've lost their minds and who are not concerned about it who actually do lose control."

Along with this fear of going crazy are the "floaty" or "unreal" feelings I described in earlier chapters. These feelings of unreality or bewilderment can also cause you to think you are going crazy. You may feel "detached" from the rest of the world or that you are "outside yourself." It can come in waves or stay for long periods of time. (This is the hardest sensation to describe -- especially to a person who has never before suffered from panic attacks!)

These feelings of unreality, though, are really nothing more than the outcome of prolonged periods of stress or anxiety. For a person in this anxious state, it is actually "normal" to feel this way. Knowing this is the cause and that you are not going crazy can bring so much relief that you will begin to feel "more real." You will gradually become more interested in the things going on around you than what is going on inside.

As with the other symptoms, feelings of unreality will not

hurt you, and the less attention given to them, the less bothersome they will be.

9) Feeling of Dread -- According to Dr. Babai, whom I quoted in an earlier chapter, one of the most common complaints from patients suffering from panic disorder is an overpowering feeling that something bad is going to happen. This feeling is different than an "instinct" or "gut feeling" in that it seems to loom about the person no matter where he or she goes. In fact, people often tend to stay in their homes for fear that if they go out this feeling will become a reality. The feelings can be vague or very specific. You may not know what bad thing will happen, or you may feel that if you get into the car, you will be killed in a terrible accident, or if you go to the bank to handle a few transactions, the bank will be robbed and you will be held hostage.

In any case, it is important to realize once again that these irrational fears are a part of the disorder. Treating yourself gently and telling yourself that you can go out and accomplish what you need to get done no matter how long it takes is the next step. You may have to ask yourself, "What is the worst that can happen?" and then be willing to say that you will go out and allow the "worst" to happen. Of course, chances are that the worst will not happen because it is an irrational fear, but it will take some time to convince yourself of this. Gradually, you will be able to move about freely without the fear that something bad will occur.

10) Feeling of Being Overwhelmed -- These particular feelings can follow a person long after the last panic attack. You are feeling fine, haven't had a symptom for a long time and your self confidence is back where it should be. So, you start making appointments and accepting responsibilities and then, suddenly you think you have overcommitted yourself and have an overwhelmed feeling. If this has happened and you feel unable to keep up with all you have agreed to do, you need to bow out gracefully and cancel a few engagements. Remember, too, that when even the littlest things seem overwhelming (like doing the dishes or washing the car), you don't have to tackle them when you are not feeling well. Nor do you have to do everything at once.

To keep the overwhelmed feelings from occurring, however, you need to be cautious as to how many commitments you make. Knowing that you tend to get overwhelmed when there are too many things going on at once should help you keep your schedule filled with only a reasonable number of commitments.

There's an acronym that I have found very helpful in remembering to keep a reasonable schedule and to keep from getting overwhelmed. The acronym is "HALT." It stands for: Never let yourself get too **h**ungry, **a**ngry, **l**onely or **t**ired.

Keeping these four areas in check serves to help maintain a positive mental outlook.

Five Steps to Triumphant Living

Learning to cope with the symptoms is one thing. But most sufferers would like to keep from getting them in the first place. Although it may not be possible to eliminate all the symptoms, you can put some principles into practice to get your life back. Following are some necessary steps that will lead to overcoming panic attacks. After you've mastered the first step, the others need occur in no particular order.

Step 1) Acceptance -- The first principle to master in your steps toward overcoming panic attacks is to truly accept the fact that you have the disorder and everything that comes along with it. This means that instead of fighting the symptoms when they arise, simply let them take their course and subside. This is in contrast to bracing yourself against the symptoms with an "I must keep this from happening" attitude.

With true acceptance, as Dr. Claire Weekes suggests, you must even welcome panic in order to practice coping with it until it no longer frightens you. The only way to overcome panic is to go through it -- and yes, you can do it!

Step 2) Positive Self Talk and Positive Thinking --
Another principle to put into practice is that of positive self talk and
positive thinking. Panic disorder sufferers can get so disoriented
from negative thought patterns and anxious feelings that they start
to believe all the negative thoughts that bombard their mind day-in
and day-out. The mind then needs to be retrained and repro-
grammed through a combination of positive thoughts and words.
(This principle is so profoundly important that I've devoted Chapter
Five to this subject).

The key is to cancel out a negative thought with a positive
one. For instance, when a negative thought like "I'll never be able
to go to the grocery store without feeling all this anxiety" comes
your way, immediately cancel it out. Replace it with something like
"I just need to be patient with myself. In time, I'll be able to move
more freely."

One of my favorite positive thoughts that I used to say and
think to myself over and over was, "I am calm, confident and
functioning normally." Even though I felt everything but calm,
confident and normal, I took the liberty to "call those things that be
not as though they are."

Some other positive thoughts to use when the negative ones
come at you are:
* I can be relaxed during any situation.
* This is just a symptom of anxiety and it will pass.
* I am in control.
* I can overcome panic disorder and learn to enjoy life
    again.
* I can handle each day one minute at a time.
* I can get through this even if I experience anxious symp-
    toms.
* I trust my body to function the way it was designed to
    function.

* I am all right. I can do this.
* I will be even better tomorrow.
* Look where I started and where I am now. I can be
    patient with myself.

It is important to create your own positive responses to negative thoughts specific to your situation. The one thing to remember when doing so is to try to always phrase these responses using affirmative language. For instance, you wouldn't say, "I am not afraid to be alone," because the word "afraid" itself is negative. Instead, saying, "I am comfortable by myself," yields more affirmation.

Step 3) Relaxation -- Learning how to relax your body is another very important aspect in overcoming anxiety and panic. Many times our bodies are tight and tense without our even realizing it. In fact, I still catch myself tensed up sometimes after spending a few hours at my computer.

You can bring your body to a more relaxed state of being in a matter of a few seconds or minutes. Taking a deep, cleansing breath in through the nose and out through the mouth can serve in a pinch. But during your early stages of recovery, you should spend about 10 to 15 minutes two to three times a day relaxing all the muscles in your body. This way, you will know what it feels like to be relaxed, and you can begin to recognize when your body tenses. Following is a relaxation technique you can use while lying on your back. It may help you to read this script into a tape recorder or have someone else whose voice is soothing read it. Then you will be able to play it whenever you are ready to relax.

Starting with your feet and toes, tighten the muscles and hold for 10 seconds, then release for 10 seconds. Repeat this five times.

Then move to your calf muscles and tighten for 10 seconds, then release for 10 seconds and repeat five times.

Now come up to your thigh muscles. Tighten the muscles

and hold for 10 seconds, then release for 10 seconds. Repeat this five times.

Now tighten the muscles in your pelvis and buttocks and hold for 10 seconds. Then release for 10 seconds and repeat five times.

Then move to the muscles in your stomach and tighten for 10 seconds, then release for 10 seconds and repeat five times.

Now tighten the muscles in your chest and hold for 10 seconds. Then release for 10 seconds and repeat five times.

Now tighten the muscles in your hands by making a fist and hold it for 10 seconds. Then release for 10 seconds and repeat five times.

Move now to your forearm. Tighten and hold for 10 seconds, then release for 10 seconds. Repeat this five times.

Then move to the muscles in your upper arm and tighten for 10 seconds, then release for 10 seconds and repeat five times.

Now tighten the muscles in your shoulders and hold for 10 seconds. Then release for 10 seconds and repeat five times

Finally, tighten the muscles in your face and jaw and hold for 10 seconds. Then release for 10 seconds and repeat five times.

Now take several deep, cleansing breaths in through your nose and out through your mouth. When you breathe in, be sure to let your stomach rise as high as possible to take in the maximum amount of air. When you breathe out, say to yourself, "I am relaxed." It may help to picture yourself in a serene setting -- perhaps by a lake or in a meadow on a beautiful summer afternoon.

After you've rested here for a few minutes, count forward from one to 10, and then arise and go on about your day.

You may find that you fall asleep at some point during the exercise. That's all right because if you are falling asleep, you are definitely relaxing.

There are many different relaxation exercises. Choose the one that is most comfortable for you or use the one I described

35

above. Just be sure to incorporate relaxation into your program of recovery.

Step 4) Desensitization -- Desensitization is another important aspect in overcoming panic disorder. This term means, in essence, gradually exposing yourself to situations and places where panic has occurred in the past. But before I get into more detail about desensitization, I want to first explain more about sensitization and panic disorder.

Dr. Weekes defines sensitization in the best way that I have seen: Sensitization is a state in which nerves are conditioned to react to stress in an exaggerated way; that is, they bring an unusually intense feeling when under stress, and at times with alarming swiftness. She goes on to say that most people have felt mild sensitization when working under pressure. Then the nerves respond too quickly and acutely to situations that would have at any other time left them unmoved.

But with severe sensitization, a person feels painfully edgy and agitated and panic comes very easily. Severe sensitization can come on suddenly or over a period of prolonged stress. It is a state of heightened awareness for the nervous system.

In any case, when attempting to gradually desensitize yourself to a specific place or situation, step one is to realize that you will most likely feel many anxious symptoms and indeed be sensitized. Give yourself permission to feel this way, knowing the only way to overcome it is to go through it.

Say, for example, you are going to attempt to walk across a bridge that has in the past brought forth fear and trepidation. Give yourself permission to experience the nervous symptoms. Before you go, spend some time doing a relaxation exercise. Be prepared as well to use positive self talk when attempting to walk across the bridge. Notice things around you to try to get your mind off the bridge. Are the flowers particularly pretty today? What about the sunshine and clouds? Are the birds singing?

36

You may want to plan to just walk to the bridge the first day and then turn around and go home. The next time you can try going half way across the bridge and turn around. Finally, you can get to the other side. If you don't make it right away, don't be too hard on yourself. At least you got as far as you did, and you can try again another day. Reinforce the positive to yourself and plan to succeed the next time around. Use these same principles to gradually desensitize yourself to other places and situations.

Step 5) Patience -- Whoever coined the phrase "patience is a virtue" was right. It takes a tremendous amount of patience with one's self to overcome panic disorder and move on to triumphant living. Although it may seem like panic disorder struck overnight, it didn't. It most likely came on after a period of prolonged stress. So you must remember that it will not disappear suddenly, either. Don't make the mistake of keeping track of how long you've been suffering from this illness. Trust me, you will get to the point where you can move about freely and without being preoccupied by your body's symptoms.

One hint that will help with the passage of time is being careful not to "fuel the fire." By this I mean not adding an "Oh my!" to your initial symptoms. "Oh my's" serve to heighten the symptoms and bring on more panic.

For example, if you are driving down the road and notice your heart beating rapidly, fueling the fire would be to say, "Oh my! My heart is racing. It must be beating over 100 beats per minute. I must be getting ready to have a panic attack. What if I have an attack while I'm driving?" etc., etc.

Instead, remain as calm as you can and resolve to allow panic to come. Practicing this will keep fear from mounting and will, with time, eventually lead to desensitized nerves.

Medication Options

I want to briefly mention that there are a variety of medication options available to sufferers from panic disorder. Great strides have been made over the past several years in the development of medications that block panic attacks.

As I mentioned earlier, according to the American Psychiatric Association, the most common treatment for the disorder is to combine medication with cognitive and behavioral therapy. In this manner, the medication serves to lessen the severity of the symptoms so the sufferer can learn more about his or her condition and acquire some coping skills. Since most of the medications do have side effects and the potential for addiction, it is recommended that the dosage be cut back as far as possible once significant improvement has been made.

Some of the most common medications used are tricyclic antidepressants (Elavil, Norpramin, Pamelor, Sinequan and Tofranil) and other drugs from the benzodiazepine group of minor tranquilizers (Atavan, Klonopin, Xanax). A newer drug, Paxil, from the class of selective serotonin re-uptake inhibitor (SSRI) antidepressants, has been found to be very effective for the treatment of panic disorder as well. Other drugs in this class are Prozac and Zoloft.

Please don't make the mistake of being hard on yourself for needing medication. Some people spend several months on a medication and others several years. Still others need medication indefinitely and are happy to just continue taking it in small doses so they can function normally.

In any case, be grateful it exists during the time you need it! It doesn't make you a weak person to need a little bit of help alleviating your symptoms. You can be sure that enough anxiety gets through the "shield" of medication to allow you to practice your coping skills and steps to triumphant living. And when the day comes that you forget to take your medicine -- be grateful once more. It's a step in the right direction.

One final word of encouragement. You can do this! You can overcome anxiety and panic attacks by practicing the coping skills and steps discussed in this chapter. But you don't have to do it alone! Jesus is there with you the whole way. Like the verse in the title of this chapter says, ''I can do all things through Christ which strengtheneth me.'' Tell yourself this many times throughout the day!

And I'll even give you a little more insight into that verse. I heard a teaching recently by Kenneth Copeland of Fort Worth, Texas, about the name Jesus Christ, and in particular the word ''Christ.'' It actually means ''the Anointed One and His anointing.'' Christ isn't just Jesus' last name! Look at the verse again, ''I can do all things through Christ which strengtheneth me.'' The word ''which'' is not a typographical error. Many people have probably thought it should read ''who strengtheneth me,'' but when you know the true meaning of the word ''Christ,'' you can see that indeed ''which'' is correct. ''I can do all things through the Anointed One and His anointing which strengtheneth me.'' Talk about overcoming power! You and Christ can do it!

Chapter Five

"Think On These Things"
Philippians 4:8

As I mentioned in Chapter Four, it is vitally important to learn to replace negative thoughts with positive thoughts and words. It may seem impossible to do this when the negative thoughts come so rapidly to the weary mind. But again, God would not tell us to do something that we are not capable of doing. And he tells us in His word in Philippians 4:8 to "think on these things," whatever is true, honest, just, pure, lovely, of good report. The Amplified Bible goes one step further and says "fix your minds on them."

The Bible also tells us in Proverbs 18 that death and life are in the power of the tongue. Therefore, we need to choose life by speaking life into our hearts and minds. The way we do this is by getting the word of God on our tongues and lips. We need to learn to think and say what God says about us in His word, not what the enemy says about us. In this way, the positive thoughts will begin to come naturally and overshadow the negative ones until they are no longer there.

This step of the healing process is what I believe made the difference in my ability to overcome anxiety and panic attacks. The medication and coping skills and steps to triumphant living were vital, but God's word is what put me over the top of the hill and on my way to recovery. God's word is health and medicine to our flesh, according to Proverbs 4:20-22. He wants us to be well. How do I know this? His word tells us how to be well. If God didn't want us to be well, why would He tell us in His word how to do it? One place where he tells us so is in the scripture mentioned above, Proverbs 4: "My son, attend to my words, incline thine ear unto my sayings. Let them not depart from thine eyes, keep them in the midst of thine heart. For they are life unto those that find them and health to all their flesh."

This scripture indicates to us that we need to not just read God's word, but to let it not depart from our eyes, and to get it into our hearts. Our terminology for this might be to "meditate" upon His word day and night. For it is in this manner that we get it into our spirit to replace the "stinking thinking" that has become the norm for many people suffering from panic disorder.

What became part of my plan for recovery was to recite out loud and then meditate upon the "healing scriptures" in the Bible. I searched in a concordance for every scripture associated with healing, life, sickness, disease, health, anxiety, worry, etc. Then I made a list of these scriptures and went about reciting and meditating or pondering upon them several times a day, every day.

Why do I feel it is so important to speak these words out loud? So you can hear yourself say it and build your faith in these words. "Faith comes by hearing and hearing by the word of God" according to Romans 10:17. You've got to have faith in the words you are speaking or you are wasting your breath. And faith comes faster when you hear yourself speak God's word.

Now, some skeptics might accuse me of being a member of the "blab it and grab it bunch" or the "name it and claim it gang," which wouldn't be all that bad because most people who have blabbed it have grabbed it or have named it and claimed it. Nonetheless, I believe, as it says in Mark 11:23, that "you have what you say." I believe that words are the most powerful tools in the uni-

41

verse and that we are where we are today because of the words we spoke yesterday. I heard a preacher say once that many of us confess or speak forth such negative things and that if we don't want them to come to pass we had better start praying for a crop failure! Isn't that the truth!?! It is like the law of sowing and reaping -- if you don't want to harvest it, don't plant it. Or, in this case, don't speak it!

Another thing I made a habit of doing was what some call positive visualization. I call it seeing yourself the way God sees you -- healed and well! I began to picture myself through the eyes of God who sees us through His Son, Jesus Christ, if we are in Him. And Jesus is not sick! He is whole and well! So instead of thinking of myself as a sufferer of panic disorder, I saw myself as a person who was whole and well -- a person who could move freely from place to place without getting sick from anxiety. I pictured myself going someplace to eat and having a wonderful time. I pictured myself going to my college courses and being able to sit through class without becoming ill. I even incorporated this into the end of my relaxation exercises, picturing these things during the time of deep breathing. Eventually, these pictures in my mind became a reality.

Following is a list of some of the scriptures I used to meditate upon and confess to help to reprogram my negative thinking patterns. I call them my "Spiritual Prescriptions." I do suggest, however, that you make it a part of your recovery process to look up healing scriptures, as well as scriptures on other topics, to help you on your road to wellness. And it might help as well to make the scriptures personal by inserting your name or the pronoun "I," "my" or "me" when applicable. For instance, Nehemiah 8:10 -- "...the joy of the Lord is my strength." Or Isaiah 54:17 -- "No weapon that is formed against me shall prosper."

Spiritual Prescription for Healing

Exodus 15:26   "And said, If thou wilt diligently hearken to the voice of the Lord thy God, and wilt do that which is right in his sight, and wilt give ear to his commandments, and keep all his statutes, I will put none of these diseases upon thee, which I have brought upon the Egyptians: for I am the Lord that healeth thee."

Psalms 91:16   "With long life will I satisfy him, and shew him my salvation."

Psalms 103:2-3   "Bless the Lord, O my soul, and forget not all his benefits: Who forgiveth all thine iniquities; who healeth all thy diseases."

Psalms 107:20   "He sent his word, and healed them, and delivered them from their destructions."

Isaiah 53:5   "But he was wounded for our transgressions, he was bruised for our iniquities: the chastisement of our peace was upon him; and with his stripes we are healed."

Jeremiah 33:6   "Behold, I will bring it health and cure, and I will cure them, and will reveal to them the abundance of peace and truth."

Matthew 8:17   "...Himself took our infirmities, and bare our sicknesses."

Matthew 9:35   "And Jesus went about all the cities and villages, teaching in their synagogues, and preaching the gospel of the kingdom, and healing every sickness and every disease among the people."

Matthew 15:30   "And great multitudes came unto him, having with them those that were lame,

43

	blind, dumb, maimed and many others, and cast them down at Jesus' feet; and he healed them."
Mark 16: 17-18	"And these signs shall follow them that believe; In my name shall they cast out devils; they shall speak with new tongues; They shall take up serpents; and if they drink any deadly thing, it shall not hurt them; they shall lay hands on the sick and they shall recover."
John 10:10	"The thief cometh not, but for to steal, and to kill, and to destroy: I am come that they might have life, and that they might have it more abundantly."
Acts 10:38	"How God anointed Jesus of Nazareth with the Holy Ghost and with power: who went about doing good, and healing all that were oppressed of the devil; for God was with him."
James 5:14-15	"Is any sick among you? let him call for the elders of the church; and let them pray over him, anointing him with oil in the name of the Lord: And the prayer of faith shall save the sick, and the Lord shall raise him up; and if he have committed sins, they shall be forgiven him."
I Peter 2:24	"Who his own self bare our sins in his own body on the tree, that we, being dead to sins, should live unto righteousness: by whose stripes ye were healed."
III John 2	"Beloved, I wish above all things that thou mayest prosper and be in health, even as thy soul prospereth."

Spiritual Prescription for Overcoming Doubt, Fear and Worry

Nehemiah 8:10   "...the joy of the Lord is your strength."

Psalms 23: 4   "Yea, though I walk through the valley of the shadow of death, I will fear no evil: for thou art with me; thy rod and thy staff they comfort me."

Psalms 27:1   "The Lord is my light and my salvation; whom shall I fear? the Lord is the strength of my life; of whom shall I be afraid?"

Psalms 34   "I will bless the Lord at all times: his praise shall continually be in my mouth. My soul shall make her boast in the Lord: the humble shall hear thereof and be glad. O magnify the Lord with me and let us exalt his name together. I sought the Lord, and he heard me, and delivered me from all my fears. They looked unto him, and were lightened: and their faces were not ashamed. This poor man cried, and the Lord heard him, and saved him out of all his troubles. The angel of the Lord encampeth round about them that fear him, and delivereth them. O taste and see that the Lord is good: blessed is the man that trusteth in him. O fear the Lord, ye his saints: for there is no want to them that fear him. The young lions do lack, and suffer hunger: but they that seek the Lord shall not want any good thing. Come, ye children, hearken unto me: I will teach you the fear of the Lord. What man is he that desireth life, and loveth many days, that he may see good? Keep thy tongue from evil, and thy lips from

speaking guile. Depart from evil, and do
good; seek peace, and pursue it. The eyes of
the Lord are upon the righteous, and his ears
are open unto their cry. The face of the Lord
is against them that do evil, to cut off the
remembrance of them from the earth. The
righteous cry, and the Lord heareth, and
delivereth them out of all their troubles. The
Lord is nigh unto them that are of a broken
heart; and saveth such as be of a contrite
spirit. Many are the afflictions of the
righteous: but the Lord delivereth him out of
them all. He keepeth all his bones: not one of
them is broken. Evil shall slay the wicked:
and they that hate the righteous shall be
desolate. The Lord redeemeth the soul of his
servants: and none of them that trust in him
shall be desolate.''

Psalms 91:10-11   ''There shall no evil befall thee, neither shall
any plague come nigh thy dwelling.''

Proverbs 3:5-6   ''Trust in the Lord with all thine heart; and
lean not to thine own understanding. In all
thy ways, acknowledge him, and he shall
direct thy paths.''

Isaiah 26:3   ''Thou will keep him in perfect peace, whose
mind is stayed on thee...''

Isaiah 41:10   ''Fear thou not; For I am with thee: be not
dismayed; for I am thy God: I will strengthen
thee; yea, I will help thee; yea, I will uphold
thee with the right hand of my righteous
ness.''

Isaiah 54:14   ''In righteousness shalt thou be established:
thou shalt be far from oppression; for thou

	shalt not fear: and from terror; for it shall not come near thee.''
Isaiah 54:17	''No weapon that is formed against thee shall prosper; and every tongue that shall rise against thee in judgment thou shalt condemn. This is the heritage of the servants of the Lord, and their righteousness is of me, saith the Lord.''
Luke 12:22,31	''...Take no thought for your life, what ye shall eat; neither for the body, what ye shall put on...But rather seek ye the kingdom of God; and all these things shall be added unto you.''
Romans 8:28	''And we know that all things work together for good to them that love God, to them who are the called according to his purpose.''
I Corinthians 2:16	''...But we have the mind of Christ.''
Philippians 4:6-7	''Be careful for nothing; but in every thing by prayer and supplication with thanksgiving let your requests be made known unto God. And the peace of God, which passeth all understanding, shall keep your hearts and minds through Christ Jesus.''
Philippians 4:19	''But my God shall supply all your need according to his riches in glory by Christ Jesus.''
Colossians 3:15	''And let the peace of God rule in your hearts...''
II Timothy 1:7	''For God hath not given us the spirit of fear; but of power, and of love, and of a sound mind.''

47

Spiritual Prescription for Power

Psalms 119:89

"For ever, O Lord, thy word is settled in heaven."

Matthew 16:19

"And I will give unto thee the keys of the kingdom of heaven: and whatsoever thou shalt bind on earth shall be bound in heaven: and whatsoever thou shalt loose on earth shall be loosed in heaven."

Matthew 18:19-20

"Again I say unto you, That if two of you shall agree on earth as touching any thing that they shall ask, it shall be done for them of my Father which is in heaven."

Mark 9:23

"...all things are possible to him that believeth."

Mark 11:23-24

"For verily I say unto you, That whosoever shall say unto this mountain, Be thou removed, and be thou cast into the sea; and shall not doubt in his heart, but shall believe that those things which he saith shall come to pass; he shall have whatsoever he saith."

Romans 10:17

"So then faith cometh by hearing, and hearing by the word of God."

Ephesians 6:16

"Above all, taking the shield of faith, wherewith ye shall be able to quench all the fiery darts of the wicked."

Philippians 4:13

"I can do all things through Christ which strengtheneth me."

James 4:7

"Submit yourselves therefore to God. Resist the devil and he will flee from you."

I John 1:9

"If we confess our sins, he is faithful and just to forgive us our sins, and to cleanse us from all unrighteousness."

I John 4:4   "...greater is He that is in you, than he that is in the world."

Revelation 12:11   "And they overcame him by the blood of the Lamb, and by the word of their testimony..."

Chapter Six

"Eat, Drink And Be Merry?"
    Luke 12:19

Like many other verses in the Bible, the one in the title of this chapter is often used in the wrong context. Most readers have heard someone say, "Eat, drink and be merry -- even the Bible tells us to do that!" People usually say this in an attempt to justify some sort of inappropriate behavior, like overindulging in alcohol or food. However, if you look more closely at Luke 12, you'll see the parable of the rich man who possessed so much that he had to build bigger barns to store it all -- and was called a fool by God. When the man thought he could sit back, take it easy and "eat, drink and be merry," God said that very night his soul would be required of him. In other words, his life on earth would be through.

We can learn a lesson from the man in this parable in that we are never to sit back, take it easy and become lazy. If we do, we, too, will be looked upon as fools by God. Instead, we need to always be alert and ready to do battle with the enemy.

I've chosen Luke 12:19 to head this chapter about taking care of our physical bodies because so often we are like the man in the parable. We think we can eat, drink and be merry or, in effect, eat whatever we want whenever we want and ignore the needs of our bodies without consequence. However, we are to do the exact opposite. We need to take care of our bodies so that we can function the way God intended us to function.

This is especially true for people who suffer from anxiety and panic attacks. Our diet and physical activity, believe it or not, play a big part in the way we think and feel. In fact, what we eat or don't eat and do or don't do can affect our level of sensitization by either calming or aggravating our anxious symptoms.

It might help us to gain a better perspective if we can learn to look at ourselves the way God made us: spirit, soul and body. We are a spirit being, we have a soul, which is comprised of our mind, will and emotions, and we live in a physical body. Our spirit is who we really are. It is that part of us that will live forever either in heaven with God, or in hell forever separated from our Creator. Our physical body is just the house that our spirit lives in while on this earth. Therefore, we are more spirit than we are flesh. We are spiritual beings having a human experience, not human beings having a spiritual experience.

Nonetheless, we are to take care of this physical body that God gave us so it will perform optimally throughout our lifetime on earth. And two of the ways we can help reduce our anxiety symptoms are by proper diet and exercise.

You Are What You Eat

I know it is an age-old saying but it is true: You are what you eat. If you eat healthy, the more likely you are to feel healthy. If you eat poorly, the more likely you are to feel poorly. Here we will look at changing some eating habits that will without a doubt improve the way you feel.

First, I want to address what I call "The Big Three:" alcohol, caffeine and sugar. These are three substances you want to avoid. In fact, you need to think of them as "poison" to your body.

Alcohol is probably the most obvious substance to avoid -- especially to Christians. The effects of alcohol on a person and his or her family are no doubt the reason the Bible tells us to stay away from it.

In Ephesians 5:18, we are instructed to "be not drunk with wine, wherein is excess, but be filled with the Spirit." Proverbs 23:31-32 tells us not to even look at wine because it will always have the "last laugh," so to speak, and it "biteth like a serpent and stingeth like an adder."

But alcohol also has an effect on the emotions. Many anxious people utilize the drug to calm themselves since it is a depressant. However, the next day, it may leave them feeling even more anxious. And since alcohol is addictive, they may find themselves needing more of it to yield the desired effect. People with anxiety or panic disorder may also be more prone to alcohol addiction, so this is definitely not the answer to their need to relax.

Finally, the combination of alcohol and antianxiety or antidepressant medications is often dangerous and may even be fatal. So it is best to avoid the substance altogether.

Now on to caffeine and sugar. I've never had much of a problem avoiding alcohol in my diet. But I'll be honest, caffeine and sugar have been and still are tough ones for me to regulate.

Most everyone knows caffeine can make you feel anxious and irritable. But did you also know that it affects your blood sugar and can cause diarrhea and an irregular heartbeat? Caffeine also dehydrates your body, leaving you feeling sluggish.

You should be aware, too, that caffeine is not only found in coffee and tea, but also in chocolate, sodas and even some diet pills and over-the-counter headache medicines. Be sure to read the nutrition labels on foods if you are trying to cut out caffeine. Also, some people experience severe headaches when they "go off" caffeine. If you are one of these people, the headaches do go away eventually. But you may need a headache remedy in the meantime. Check with your doctor if you have a serious concern or if the headaches persist for more than a week.

As for sugar, you will probably have to do everything you can to eliminate it from your diet, as well. You may be saying,

"Come on, first alcohol, then caffeine -- don't make me give up my sugar, too!" Yes, the sugar has to go. Why? Because it makes your blood sugar levels go up and down. For instance, when you ingest sugar, your blood sugar level rises and the pancreas then balances out your system by producing insulin. But sometimes the pancreas produces too much insulin, and then you are out of balance once again. And when your sugar is too low, you can have the symptoms of anxiety or a panic attack because your body releases adrenaline in an effort to bring that blood sugar level back up.

So do try to eliminate sugar from your diet. But be patient because it takes time to wean yourself off sweets.

Now, moving on to general diet and nutrition, there are many excellent resources available to tell you how to eat right and obtain all the nutrients that make up a balanced diet. Some are even designed by Christians who tell us how to eat the way God would want us to eat to ward off disease and infection. I will not try to be a nutrition expert, but after reading several articles on the subject, I know it is safe to say that some of our symptoms can be brought on by not eating properly.

Take the time to go to your local library or Christian or other bookstore and read up on the latest findings in nutrition. I think you'll be amazed, as I was, at how poorly America on the whole eats. You will also find that taking vitamin and mineral supplements is an absolute necessity to obtain essential elements that can no longer be found in the foods we consume.

And along with eating right is drinking right. It is vitally important for us to drink at least eight to 10 eight-ounce glasses of water a day to flush the toxins from our bodies. This also keeps us from retaining fluid, which contributes to bloating and could mean a few extra pounds to carry around.

In general, eating appropriately from the four food groups, cutting out alcohol, caffeine and sugar, and drinking a lot of water will help to bring your body to a healthier state.

Healthy Body, Healthy Mind

Exercise goes hand in hand with proper diet. You not only need to eat appropriately but also to get the proper amount of activity in order to feel your best, both physically and mentally.

Exercise causes the body to produce endorphins, compounds that are secreted in the brain that make you feel good (runner's high), as well as help to control the way you think and respond. Exercise will also help you obtain your ideal body weight -- or at least get you closer to the normal range for your age, height and bone structure.

To determine the amount of physical activity that is appropriate for you, consider joining your local YMCA, YWCA or other health club. These locations usually have qualified trainers on staff who can customize a fitness program especially for you. Such a program will probably combine aerobic (activity that conditions the heart and lungs by increasing the efficiency of oxygen intake by the body) and non-aerobic activity and will allow you to take advantage of the latest in workout equipment. From using stairmasters to treadmills and everything in between, you will be able to get in shape and maybe make a new friend or two while you are at it.

Another option is to work with your physician, whom you should contact before beginning any physical fitness program. He or she can construct a plan appropriate for you and your goals. This might include walking, jogging, bicycling, doing aerobic videos or perhaps playing on your church's softball or basketball team. And it doesn't have to cost a great deal. You should invest in proper shoes, however, so as not to harm your feet or knees.

Whichever course you choose, be sure to start out slow and with realistic goals. Remember once again that your body didn't get into this predicament overnight, so don't expect a perfectly shaped and toned physique overnight, either.

Try to have fun while you exercise. Include a friend or family member when you can. It'll do wonders for your motivation!

Chapter Seven

"We Are All Part Of One Body"
Ephesians 4:4

As the title of this chapter indicates, when one member of the body of Christ suffers, we all suffer. It only makes sense, then, that when a person suffers from a problem such as anxiety and panic disorder, it affects those around him or her. In fact, victims' family members are often just as frustrated as the person suffering with the symptoms. And what a family does or doesn't do can have a big impact on how quickly a person recovers from the disorder.

My experience with how the illness affected those around me was quite common. As I related in an earlier chapter, my husband, Jeff, reacted with denial, anger and frustration. This was born out of the fact that he did not want to believe his new wife had indeed "contracted" a mental illness. Anxiety and panic attacks were not as openly discussed back in the '80s as they are today. It was easier for him to just pretend it wasn't there and try to act as though things were still "normal."

Anger and frustration settled in when it was apparent the problem was not just going to go away. Jeff realized that because my life was hindered, his was, too. And Jeff had always been a person who got his own way and was very active. Patience was not one of his characteristics, but it is something that a sufferer from panic disorder desperately needs from family and friends around him or her.

I can remember Jeff becoming angry because I was unable to keep up with his desire to be on the go. In one instance, after a day of classes at the university, I was not physically or emotionally capable of handling a Friday night high school football game. He told me I was acting like I was 81 instead of 21 and that he was not sitting home on a Friday night. He went into a rage and ended up throwing a lamp across the room and my medication in the waste-basket. Then he went to the football game and I stayed home, retrieved my medicine from the trash, and cried.

On another occasion, we were celebrating New Year's Eve by going to dinner with friends. Sure enough, that is when an episode of diarrhea decided to attack. Luckily, it hit before we left, and I was able to take an over-the-counter remedy to get it under control. I do remember his comments of frustration, though, as I was writhing in pain: ''Why is it that every time we plan to go somewhere, you get the runs?'' I explained to him that I didn't want to get sick but it was just something I dealt with. After more angry words and about half a bottle of Kaopectate, I was able to accompany him to dinner with our friends, although I didn't eat.

Like Jeff, spouses of individuals suffering from panic disor-der often find themselves ''trapped'' in a frustrating situation. Although his reaction did not help my condition and in fact prob-ably hindered it, his response is common: The victim is having symptoms and the loved one wants to help ''make it all go away.'' When he or she realizes there is little that can be done, anger often results. There are, however, a few steps that can help make it easier for the loved one to deal with the illness.

First, the victim's loved ones should learn as much as pos-sible about anxiety and panic disorder. With an open mind, they should ask the sufferer to relate everything he or she knows about the illness. Then, they should read about it in books from the library or pamphlets from the doctor's office. The more friends and family understand the disorder, the more they will understand what the sufferer is going through.

The second thing is to learn to participate in activities without the person who has the illness. If the sufferer suddenly backs out of an event, it is not cruel to go on and attend without him or her. In fact, it lets the person know that life is still going on. And it keeps the family member from feeling isolated or controlled by the illness.

Third, the family member must realize that, in most cases, he or she is not the one causing the anxiety and panic. It is senseless for the spouse or loved one to feel guilty about the sufferer's illness. Such a reaction only adds stress to what is already a difficult situation.

In some cases, however, the sufferer's environment is the major precipitator for the onset of panic disorder. As I mentioned in an earlier chapter, I believe I had a genetic predisposition for anxiety and panic. This belief is because a number of people in my father's family have dealt with anxiety or depression. But I didn't feel that my childhood or the environment in which I was raised made it more likely for me to succumb to the illness. I do, though, feel that the environment I was in with Jeff created the right condition for the onset of the disorder.

What makes me think that? The fact that we were two very different personality types was a big factor. I know a lot of married couples have opposite personalities -- after all, opposites attract, right? But Jeff was a hyper person, like I said before, very active and always on the go. He was obnoxious and emotionally immature. My sister put it best by saying he was a 10-year-old trapped in a 23-year-old's body. To give you an example, on one of the few occasions he attended church with me, he put jelly beans in the offering envelope!

I am not saying all this to paint a nasty picture of Jeff. After all, I married him. He was handsome, outgoing, funny and charming. He was also carefree and liked to have fun. Looking back, I suppose that was what attracted me most. Jeff never worried about anything and did his part to enjoy life, whereas I had always taken life so seriously.

But there was a side to Jeff that I had looked past when we were dating: He was by nature a very angry individual. Mix that with the fact that he wasn't a Christian and it spelled big problems for us.

Jeff admitted he had difficulty controlling his emotions and his temper. However, without the Holy Spirit inside him, there was very little hope of improvement in this area. Jeff's lack of spirituality spread to other areas, too -- mainly his total refusal to be around anything that was even remotely related to the Lord or church. I believe, as it says in John 3:19, this was due to the fact that darkness hates the light because light exposes the darkness for what it truly is. Jeff vehemently opposed my spending time with my family or Christian friends. He also hassled me every time I wanted to attend Bible study or church and did everything he could to make it difficult for me to play on the church softball team. When I gave in to his wishes, I was essentially starving my spirit. Coupled with the fact that I was predisposed to having problems handling stress, this set up the perfect environment to bring on panic attacks and anxiety. Once the condition surfaced, he was incapable of accepting it or of doing anything to help me.

Because I was not getting the love and support I needed from Jeff, I turned to my mother and father. I talked to my mom on the phone nearly every night. She walked me through some of my irrational fears and helped me to see things through the proper perspective. Sometimes she would patiently repeat herself over and over until I felt confident that I could go on.

Dad offered valuable insight into the problems I was experiencing and continued to assure me that I would get better. It must have been so difficult for the two of them as parents to see their daughter suffering...especially because Dad had gone through the same thing so recently. I can remember not wanting to talk about my symptoms too much with my father for fear it would trigger another episode for him. But he would reassure me that wouldn't happen and that he was just doing what he could to help me through a difficult time.

There are a few things other than simply talking and listening to the sufferer that spouses and family members can do to help. One of these things is to accompany him or her to the doctor. Not only will this help the family member learn more about the illness, but it will also show support to the sufferer. The family member may also pick up on something the doctor says that the patient may have missed or remind the patient of questions to ask the doctor. So many issues are often crammed into a half-hour or hour visit that this usually proves very helpful.

A second thing is to encourage the person to practice his coping skills, relaxation exercises and steps for overcoming the disorder. This includes, as one spouse of a panic disorder sufferer says, encouraging the victim to continue with planned activities (desensitization) if possible. At times, she still must do things by herself and doesn't make a big deal out of sudden changes in plans, but this gentle, non-threatening encouragement often makes a big difference.

She also says that she's learned to divert her husband's attention to something else when he can't seem to do so himself. Lightening up the situation can be extremely beneficial.

Also, family members shouldn't hesitate to help the sufferer study scripture verses to use against the symptoms and pray for him.

Finally, whatever family members do, they must remember to be patient with the sufferer. Every person recovers at a different pace, and it is important that each victim find the pace that is comfortable. Only then does true recovery occur.

The sufferer can also help family members in various ways.

Perhaps the biggest way to help a family member is by not putting undue stress on him or her. For instance, if there is some chore or errand that you can handle or tackle on your own, by all means do it so as not to put an extra burden on the family member. Or, if you can accompany a loved one somewhere with only a few minor symptoms, go! There will be plenty of instances when you really can't tackle something or go somewhere. Use your best judgment and ask for help or decline only when absolutely necessary.

Second, try to obtain support via people other than your spouse or family. If you have a strong network of Christian friends, you may want to lean on them every now and then. It is important to talk to other people so that when you are with your family you can talk about something other than your illness.

Finally, be patient with your family, as they are being patient with you. They are bound to get frustrated from time to time when their own patience wears thin or when they don't understand something you are going through. But above all, be sure to respond in love -- remember what Proverbs 15:1 says -- "a soft answer turneth away wrath."

Chapter Eight

"And Let The Peace Of God Rule In Your Hearts"
Colossians 3:15

One of the most difficult things for a person suffering from panic disorder and anxiety to do is make decisions. Even if he takes all the information he has available to him and tries to make the best and most informed decision possible, he may still find he second guesses himself and starts "what-if-ing" again. "What if the decision he makes is the wrong one?" "What if he makes a mistake?" He may also find he asks several people for advice and needs to be reassured over and over again before he makes a decision. Or, he may ask someone for advice regarding a decision and receive input, only to go and do the exact opposite of what the person suggested.

By far the biggest reason for indecision is the fear of making the wrong choice. However, wavering in ambivalence is far worse than simply making up your mind. And it can be tormenting to you and those around you. You can take some simple steps to help make the decision-making process a little less stressful. But ultimately, you do have to take that final step and make up your mind.

The first step when making any decision is to pray and ask the Lord for guidance. You may find yourself saying your decision seems so menial that it couldn't possibly matter to God. But believe it or not, He does care even about the little things. If it is important to you, it is important to your Heavenly Father.

61

Okay, so you've asked the Lord for guidance, now how is He supposed to answer? Not many people hear God's reply in an audible voice. Therefore, the answer has to come in another fashion. He may answer you through another person who didn't even know your situation. God may choose to speak to him or her during prayer time with a word for you. The Lord may also speak to you through something you read during your daily devotion or meditation. Or He may speak to you through that still, small voice that you've come to recognize as His. Whatever you do, don't ''put God in a box.'' He is the Creator and has been known to have very creative methods of getting answers to His people.

The second step in the decision-making process is to give it the ''scripture test.'' Check the scriptures to see what God has already said about the subject. Now, this step will not apply to all decisions because some things aren't in the scriptures. For instance, if you are considering whether to accept a certain job offer, there won't be a clear-cut answer in the Bible that says, ''Thou shalt take the position with XYZ Company.'' But you can discern by looking at underlying Biblical principles. Will the position require you to compromise any of God's commandments? Will you still be able to attend church regularly, or will you be working 80 or 90 hours a week? Will you have to compromise and spend less time with your family?

Then there are other questions that have an answer clearly defined in the scriptures. For example, let's say you are trying to decide whether to accept a marriage proposal with someone who is not a Christian. That answer is clearly given in 2 Corinthians 6:14 -- ''Be ye not unequally yoked together with unbelievers.'' (This is one I should have heeded back when I was 20). Notice, it doesn't say, ''unless you are trying to get them saved.'' It says ''be ye not.'' Also, in Amos 3:3 -- ''Can two walk together except they be agreed.'' And God will never contradict His word. He can't. So even if you think God wants you to marry this person, there is no way He will contradict His word. You can be sure that if it doesn't line up with scripture, it is not of God.

Third, gather all the information you can and be as informed as possible before you make any decision. Depending on the magnitude of the choice, you may have to do a little fact-finding or research. But ultimately, the more knowledge you have about the situation, the better the position you will be in to decide.

The fourth step in the decision-making process is to talk to a trusted Christian friend or two. Hopefully you have a spouse or person close to you that you can talk to openly about any and all choices with which you are faced. Sometimes it helps just to lay it all out on the table with someone who is on the outside looking in. They may be able to see things much more clearly and objectively and help to make your choice more definitive. However, don't pull too many people into this process, or you are likely to get several different answers and be more confused than when you began.

Finally, as the verse in the title of this chapter says, "Let peace be your umpire." If you feel at peace in your spirit about a particular choice, it is likely of God. Conversely, if you have an unsettled feeling in your spirit, this is most likely a sign that it is not of God. Some people call this an "instinct" or "gut feeling," but it is really the Holy Spirit communicating with you and prompting you to stay in line with the will of God.

After you've gone though these five steps, it is time to make your decision. You need to make the best possible choice based on the knowledge and information you have at the time. And one thing that might bring you a bit of comfort and rest is knowing you can always change your mind and change directions if it doesn't work out. However, you can only concentrate on one path at a time and know that God is with you each step of the way. He is not hovering above the fork in the road waiting for you to choose the left or the right and then there to say, "Well, you picked the wrong one; I'm out of here." Instead, He's there with you, and if you make an error, He can still work in your life.

On my road to recovery, I was faced with many decisions. The first major one came up in 1991. I needed to decide whether to take a full-time job in my field of public relations. It would mean driving 30 minutes each way to work an 8 a.m. to 4:30 p.m. job at a company for which I had been freelancing for the past year and a half. The pay was good and the benefits were excellent. And, with the way the position opened up, I knew I was clearly in the right place at the right time. Another freelancer who shared the public relations and marketing responsibilities with me had started her own agency. That left her part of the work with no one to complete it. The easiest way to remedy the situation was to combine all the duties into one full-time position and offer it to me.

One of the things that made me question whether or not to take the job was that it would mean my giving up the flexible schedule that freelancing provided. Until that point, I had been setting my own hours, working about 20 to 30 hours a week. I was careful to plan my schedule around Jeff, who was now working afternoons at a correctional facility, as well as odd shifts at the local police department.

Another thing that concerned me was my condition with panic disorder. I seriously doubted whether my body could handle working a 40-hour week. And how on earth would I be able to get up at 6 a.m. every day when Jeff didn't get home until 11:30 p.m.? Would I be able to do it or would they find out I wasn't ''normal'' and that I had panic disorder? Of course, I was forgetting to reassure myself with the fact that I would be going to familiar surroundings. I was used to driving to the company three times a week already, and I was accustomed to the people and the work as well. But that was when I was still training my brain to focus on the positive.

Well, unfortunately, Jeff didn't quite understand my reasons for wanting to remain a freelancer. He was adamant that I take the position, citing the full-time salary as his primary reason. He accused me of being lazy if I didn't take it, saying that if it was being offered, I should accept.

And accept it I did, although I felt that the Lord might want me to remain a freelancer because it lent itself more readily to the lifestyle of a Christian wife and, eventually, mother. But I once again succumbed to Jeff's pressure and joined the force of full-time working women.

The first day on the job, I spent about 45 minutes in the restroom when my irritable bowel syndrome decided to act up. I thought that if this was a sign of how things were going to go, then I was in for trouble. But much to my amazement, I did fine at work. For the first time ever, our department actually published a monthly newsletter that went out each month. And we also successfully produced a quarterly publication that went out four times that year! Everyone was happy with my work, and I was pleased to be able to perform without any problems. I remember saying to the doctor, "I'm faking my way through it." Her reply was, "You're not faking anything. You're doing it!" I guess I was.

However, it was difficult at home because of Jeff's afternoon rotating schedule. He would work 3 to 11 p.m., seven days on and two days off, then eight days on and four days off. His days off would be Tuesdays and Wednesdays for the two-day and Friday through Monday for the four-day. So very rarely was he home during the evenings after my days at work. I would try to stay awake until 11:30 p.m. to at least talk to him for a while when he got home. But that was hard and would leave me feeling very tired the next day at work. Most weekends, he slept until 11 a.m. or noon, then awoke and got ready for work. We didn't see each other much because he also worked a shift or two a week at the police department.

During this time, I began to walk and do aerobics with a neighbor of mine. I also spent time reading, attending Bible study and a women's support group at the church. Throughout the course of this support group I learned I had been exhibiting codependent behavior in my relationship with Jeff. I had actually been acting one way or another to keep him from going into a rage, or in essence, to keep him "fixed." I would try to do or not do things to keep from "setting him off." This included not visiting my family, not spending time with Christian friends, not attending church, and not going to softball practice or Bible study or basically anywhere, especially on his days off. Gradually, I learned through counseling with my pastor and attending the support group, that this was not healthy behavior. I then began to slowly stand up to Jeff and actually do things knowing what the consequences might be. Not to do so was only enabling him to continue his controlling, manipulative behavior.

Please don't take what I've related here the wrong way. I am not against being a submissive wife, and I know what the Bible says about winning an unsaved husband to the Lord. But our relationship needed much more than Jeff's becoming a Christian. A lot of the actions I took were based on what our relationship needed to become healthy -- Christian or not. And I firmly believed this is what it would take for our marriage to survive. I also believed that eventually Jeff would give his heart to the Lord and become a Christian.

Throughout the next few months, though, Jeff became increasingly verbally and emotionally abusive. His control over me was not what it once was and he was not at all pleased. He subsequently began spending time with some new friends he had met at the correctional facility. Usually this meant a morning of golf or an evening of bars, cards or pool. But it always meant drinking. An occasion or two had him out until 3 or 4 a.m.

Finally, I told Jeff that we needed to get good Christian counseling because our marriage was in trouble. Of course, he resisted so I attended counseling with a Christian marriage counselor assigned to us by his insurance. I figured I could learn some things that I could do and at least do my part to help improve the relationship.

Things were not improving, however, and it was increasingly difficult to be together. I soon found myself looking at my second major decision: whether to file for separation. After much prayer and consideration, I leaned toward separation. I felt that if we had some time apart, Jeff would realize how serious our situation was. But I struggled with this because I was really trying not to do anything that was displeasing to God. In no way did I want a divorce, but I knew that emotionally I couldn't go on with a man like this. So I thought that in order to save the marriage, I needed to get his attention and wake him up -- kind of a *Love Must Be Tough* course of action.

But I wasn't quite ready for a separation and I thought I'd give the counseling idea one more try. Surprisingly, Jeff agreed. We went to the counseling session and I mentioned that I had been thinking about a separation. Well, that was a mistake! Right away, Jeff flew off the handle and didn't even let me explain that now that we were counseling, maybe we could avoid that whole ordeal. When Jeff asked the counselor what he thought about a separation, the counselor replied it might be what our marriage needed. Then Jeff went berserk. He got up and shouted some unmentionable obscenities and stormed out of the counselor's office, taking the car keys and locking them in the car. He went next door and called for a friend to pick him up at the root beer stand up the street. I, meanwhile, had to call AAA and have them come and unlock my car.

By the time I got home, Jeff was already gone. He had taken all his clothes and driven to a friend's house. That night was the most peaceful night I had had in months.

But the peacefulness ended the next day when Jeff called and asked me to pick up him and his buddy. They had gotten stranded somehow after a night out at the bars. I went and got them and Jeff proceeded to talk me into having him come back home. His episode included tears and pleading and promises to attend counseling and start going to church -- but not my church. So I gave in and he brought all his things home.

Our relationship actually improved over the next several months. We went to a church together on the Sundays when he could get himself out of bed. The marriage counseling never panned out, nor did his promises to get help for his temper. But we did attend a couples weekend at the church where we were going. So all in all, I was satisfied.

However, as I mentioned in an earlier chapter, without a true commitment to the Lord and the Holy Spirit in his heart, lasting change wasn't possible. I remember my pastor telling me that I let Jeff come home too soon and that he would be back to his old tricks within six months. Once again, Pastor was right! About six months later, Jeff began to run around with the single guys from work again and his temper and drinking resumed.

After he moved out once more for a short period of time, he came back and said that was it. If I wanted us to be separated, I was the one who would have to move. After about six weeks and more thought and prayer, I did just that. But not without a lot of turmoil because of what the Bible says about divorce. Once again, though, a healthy marriage was still my goal and I was convinced that this was the only way. I went through the decision-making process and had peace about it. Shortly thereafter, too, I received a prophecy at church and was told I was "in direct contiguity with the Lord." So I knew things were going to be all right no matter what happened.

It took some getting used to -- having an apartment of my own was a big step to take. People with panic disorder don't like change, but I kept telling myself it had to be done and that the end result would be worth it. When I purchased anything for the apartment, I made sure I'd be able to use it back at the duplex "when Jeff and I got back together."

Over the next few months Jeff and I talked all the time and I continued to counsel with the marriage counselor and my pastor. I tried not to do anything that would grieve the Lord. But Jeff continued with his nights out at the bars and didn't seem to want to get serious about anything. He would stay out until all hours of the morning and would hide his car when he was home. I suspected he was seeing other women, but I could never prove it. The verbal and emotional abuse also continued and at one point I was forced to call the police. Jeff insisted that the anger was my fault for what I was putting him through.

Two months turned into six and we found ourselves legally divorced instead of just legally separated. My heart was sick because it seemed like my plan had backfired. But I drew hope from a "Focus on the Family" radio program I heard one day featuring couples who had remarried after having been divorced. I continued to pray that we could be reconciled even after all we'd been through.

About six months after the divorce, it seemed as though my prayers were being answered. Jeff attended a Christian men's retreat with his former boss from the plumbing company. He returned with what appeared to be a sincere heart and said he had turned his life over to the Lord and that things were really going to change for us. He admitted to having been unfaithful to me through our period of separation and I didn't push for anything prior to that because I didn't want to know. But I forgave him and said we would take it slowly. That was in October and it was tough but things seemed to be getting better. We even counseled with the pastor of the church that hosted the retreat.

Then in January my hopes were shattered for good. He came to my apartment and told me the news: A girl he had dated when we were separated and then again when we were divorced was four weeks pregnant. And it, too, was my fault, or so he stated, because I wanted to take things too slowly.

I actually contemplated overlooking this, too, because Jeff said that although he'd made a mistake, he still wanted to be with me. I wasn't sure if I could handle all this but we said we wouldn't make any decisions right away. But shortly thereafter, they found out they were having twins and that about did it for me. I didn't feel led to stay with a man who was having twins with another woman. And I didn't feel it was God's best for me either. But I knew that He was guiding me and I had the assurance of knowing I was "in direct contiguity with Him."

Did I make the wrong decision by getting a divorce? Would I do it all again? No and yes. And let me tell you this: No one hates divorce as much as a person who is going through it. Because of what the Bible says about divorce in 1 Corinthians 7, it is not a subject to be taken lightly. However, in 1 Corinthians 7:13 it says, "And the woman which hath an husband that believeth not, and if he be pleased to dwell with her, let her not leave him." Further down, verse 15 ends with "...but God hath called us to peace." Clearly, Jeff was not "pleased" to dwell with me. This was evidenced by his behavior and outbursts of temper and rage. And because God wants peace for us, I felt I was not under bondage in this case.

Also, as I mentioned, I followed the steps for making a decision. I asked the Lord for guidance, gave it the scripture test, and gathered all the information I could about the situation. I spoke with Christian counselors, my pastor and family, and I felt at peace about the decision I made. I even had confirmation from a prophet and through a word from the assistant pastor. He said that when he was praying about my situation the Lord told him He had something better for me and that "enough is enough."

I believe one of the reasons I went through this divorce was because I did not think through the decision to marry Jeff in the first place. I made the decision too quickly and did not heed the advice of those around me. I also did not pray about it and did not take into consideration what the Lord said in His word about marrying an unbeliever.

It is critical to thoroughly think through each decision you make -- especially those of major, life-changing importance. Sometimes it is not so easy to simply change your mind if you make a mistake. But one thing is for certain: If you do err, God is still there with you and will still work in your life as He did in mine.

Chapter Nine:

*"How Much More Shall Your Father Give Good Things
To Them That Ask?"*   *Matthew 7:11*

God is so good! Little did I know how badly I would need a
full-time position when I was wrestling with the decision of whether
to take it. But God knew what I would have need of -- good pay,
benefits, job security -- and provided it at just the right time!

God also knew of my need for companionship. Like most
panic disorder sufferers, I did not do well on my own. I was never
alone, because the Lord was always there with me, but I was lonely
-- there's a difference.

Some time after the divorce I received another word from
the Lord through a prophetic minister at our church. The Lord said
there would be a man coming into my life that was tall in spirit,
dark and handsome. But first I had to "clean out my closets" and
get rid of everything from the past.

Now I had been dating a Christian gentleman I met through
work, and he was tall and handsome. But he was already in my life
so it was apparent he was not the one to whom the Lord was
referring. Plus he had two children from a previous marriage and I
didn't feel at peace about forming a long-term relationship with
him. It just didn't seem to be God's best for me. So that friendship
ended and I began to be on the lookout for this dark and handsome
man who wasn't necessarily tall physically, but was in spirit. I
"cleaned out my closets" and removed all the mementos and items

that reminded me of my marriage to Jeff.

Not long after that, I ran into an acquaintance of Jeff's and mine. His name was Randy and he was quite a character -- but not a Christian by any means. It never even crossed my mind that he could be this tall, dark and handsome man that God had told me about. But we would go to dinner and enjoyed country line dancing and just generally had a good time. Neither of us was even considering a long-term relationship. We were just friends.

Eventually I invited Randy to church and he eagerly accepted the invitation. The Cathedral of Life is a full-gospel church, so the free style of praise and worship and praying and speaking forth God's word in tongues was much different from the church in which Randy grew up. But he was open-minded and liked the word of God he heard preached. It wasn't long before he began attending services regularly and made friends with other men in the church. He joined the men's softball team that spring and shortly thereafter turned his life over to the Lord. Then it dawned on me that he was the man God sent to me. Within a few short months we were talking about marriage. But before I was going to enter into another marriage commitment I wanted to be absolutely certain this was God's will for our lives. Our church has mandatory premarital counseling if a couple wants to be married by one of our pastors. So, before we even announced our intentions and before Randy asked my father for my hand in marriage, we attended a few counseling sessions. After much prayer and consideration, we were positive it was God's will for our lives that we be together. And so we were engaged in August of 1993 and planned to marry in May of 1994.

Much to my amazement, my anxiety and panic symptoms were minimal during the time Randy and I dated and planned our wedding. I am convinced that this lack of symptoms was because I had a perfect peace about the entire relationship. When I told Randy about my condition and the fact that I was on medication, he was very loving and said he would do everything he could not to create more anxiety for me. He said he wanted our home, wherever it may be, to be a peaceful environment where we could relax and enjoy each other. And he has the laid-back temperament to follow through and do just that. Once again -- God knew exactly what I needed!

Because of Randy's easy-going attitude toward just about everything and his undying support, I was able to make three major transitions with only mild symptoms. These transitions were another change in residence, a change in doctors and a change in medication.

The first one -- a change in residence -- was an obvious necessity now that Randy and I were planning to marry. We couldn't both live in my tiny one-bedroom apartment and Randy had just sold his three-bedroom ranch and moved back with his father. So we began house hunting. Once again, the Lord provided exactly what we needed and He gave us the desires of our hearts while He was at it: a modest split level in a rural area that had a lot of promise. It needed some work, but the location was ideal. We didn't know where the money would come from to do all the fixing up -- especially with a wedding fast approaching -- but we were sure God would handle that, too.

The second major transition was switching doctors. Due to a change in insurance plans, I could no longer see Dr. Grewal. Things were going so well and I had had no severe symptoms, so why did the change in insurance have to go and mess everything up? Well, needless to say, just the thought of switching doctors brought on some mild anxiety. But Dr. Grewal worked with me to select another good psychiatrist. We chose Dr. Massood R. Babai, chairman of the Department of Psychiatry at Summa/St. Thomas Hospital in Akron.

As I mentioned earlier when talking about anticipatory anxiety, things seldom turn out as bad as you think they will. All the worst thoughts had crossed my mind: "What if Dr. Babai can't help me like Dr. Grewal?" "What if I don't like him?" "What if I start getting worse again?" Well, needless to say, none of these came to pass. In fact, I really liked Dr. Babai and he has been my doctor ever since. But one of the first things he did for me was the third major transition during this time frame: He changed my medications. Imagine the horror -- not just switching doctors, but switching medications, too!

Dr. Babai wanted to get me off Xanax and onto another antianxiety drug that had fewer side effects and was not as habit-forming. That drug was Klonopin. Klonopin, he explained, had a longer half-life. This meant it would stay in my system much longer before dropping to 50 percent effectiveness. By the time that happened, I would have most likely taken another dose. This second dose, in turn, would also stay in my system longer before reducing to 50 percent effectiveness. In essence then, I would most likely have even fewer symptoms of anxiety and panic and would not be able to tell as readily when the medication was wearing off.

So I tapered off the Xanax and made the switch to Klonopin...but not without having some more mild anxiety and panic symptoms. "What if the Klonopin didn't work?" "What if it made me feel weird?" Those questions were replaced with more positive thoughts: "What if it did work like the doctor said?" "What if I had no symptoms at all anymore?" And once again, the Lord was working in the midst of the situation. What I thought was something negative was actually a blessing in disguise. With the Klonopin I felt like a new person. I didn't have any symptoms for the most part and would actually forget when it was time to take the medication. With Xanax, I always knew when it was time to take the next dose -- my body would tell me with hot flashes and anxious symptoms. Once again, to my amazement, God had taken what I thought were negative situations and turned them into something very positive. When would I quit being amazed and realize this is just how God works?

Now then, as for fixing up the house and paying for our wedding and honeymoon, God had a plan for that, too. Randy, who is part Cherokee Indian, enjoyed making Native American crafts. But he mostly made them as gifts or to keep and decorate his walls. When a friend of mine saw some of the items he made, she suggested he start attending some of the local craft shows and artisan fairs to make some money from his hobby. That hobby turned into a nice little side business of authentic Native American crafts and paid for much of the home repairs, wedding and honeymoon. It is amazing what can happen when the Lord decides to bless a bunch of sticks and rocks!

When our wedding finally arrived it was the wedding of our dreams. Nothing fancy -- in fact it was a country-western theme wedding complete with cowboy boots, hats and gingham dresses. Pastor even wore boots and a bolo tie under his robe! It was a true celebration after which we honeymooned in Texas.

But the trials and tribulations of life didn't even wait for us to get back from our honeymoon. My sister was house- and dog-sitting for us and had received a message for me to call my OB-GYN doctor as soon as possible. Apparently one of my routine test results came back suspicious. I called the doctor from Texas and was informed that I needed to come in and be re-checked because an abnormal growth appeared on the last test. So I made the appointment for the day we returned home. Randy and I immediately prayed that nothing serious would come of this and that I would be fine.

After another test and biopsy, we learned that what I had contracted was linked to a problem from which my ex-husband had suffered. What he had was sexually transmitted. How timely to find out now that indeed Jeff had been unfaithful while we were married. But I was suffering the consequences! Thankfully, the problem hadn't progressed any further and we were able to correct it with surgery. Once again, though, I found myself going through something because of Jeff and having to exercise my faith and forgiveness.

Soon after the wedding I learned how different it is to live with someone of Randy's temperament. It is wonderful! He is not only understanding about anxiety and panic disorder and looking out for me, but he also understands the differences between men and women in general. For instance -- a woman's need to talk! He is forever encouraging me to spend time with other women to ''get my words in.'' This is his way of dealing with the fact that women have the need to speak about 20,000 more words a day than men. I think it's also his way of keeping me from driving him crazy!

In all seriousness, God gave me a man who now looks out for me physically, spiritually and emotionally. And it makes all the difference in the world -- especially to someone who suffers from anxiety and panic disorder. Randy is not perfect by any means. He loses his temper occasionally and gets frustrated with having to be so patient and delicate with me. But his emotional and spiritual maturity guide him and help him relate to me.

Little did we know that we would both need the patience of Job with what would come at us during the next three years. And I truly believe that the reason I handled it so well is because of the change in medication and the loving, understanding home environment Randy creates for me.

Shortly after our marriage there was a major change in the philosophy of the company where I worked. The shift in focus went from the employee and creating a positive work environment to producing a perfect product that yielded large profits. Much of this was due to the demands customers were placing on the company, but many good employees were lost in the process. I was one of them. Employees were expected to work more than 40 hours per week to keep up with the workload but were not given additional compensation. If you didn't stay late during the evening or come in on a Saturday, it was frowned upon. Don't get me wrong, I believed in working hard for my boss -- the Bible instructs us to do so. But I also believed that first comes God, then your spouse or family, and after that, work. I felt my philosophy didn't fit with the company's philosophy any longer, so I began looking for employment elsewhere. God was again watching out for me and He opened up a position for me at a place where my values were welcomed: a private, Catholic, all-girls school.

At the same time I began this new position in public relations and marketing, Randy started a new job with the state as a parole officer. But something else happened that day that would change our lives forever: We would learn that Randy's mother had terminal cancer. We saw great miracles along the way, though, during her nine months left here on earth. One of these miracles was the strength God gave us to sustain us through this period. Thank goodness we knew Beverly was going to heaven! Just prior to her diagnosis, she had accepted the Lord into her life at a "Heaven's Gates and Hell's Flames" production at our church. Talk about just in time!

A few other trials tested us during the same time...one of which was a strange infection that put Randy in the hospital for four days. He had somehow contracted a staph infection in his knee that made it swell to three times the normal size. He says he was never so sick in his entire life and I believe him. Not only was he hospitalized, but he was also off work four weeks. I'm sure if he could have chosen the time to have this happen it would not have been when it did. One of the biggest craft shows took place during the time he was hospitalized and our Dalmatians had just had puppies the month before. If you ever want to test your patience -- try having nine dogs in the house!

Anyway, God graciously saw us through the rough spots as we knew He would. And again, thanks to my husband's wonderful, loving attitude, gentleness and extreme patience, I was symptom free for the most part. During times when I would let myself get overwhelmed and stressed, Randy did all he could to lift excessive burdens from me and make my life a little easier. I believe it is absolutely essential to choose a mate like this if you deal with anxiety and panic.

After Randy's mother's death in 1996, Randy and I decided life was too precious to spend working all the time. Beverly's death really made us realize how important family is and we decided to begin a family of our own. But we didn't want to do that with my working full-time outside the home. So, we made arrangements for me to freelance again. It was hard to have the faith to believe I could make enough money on my own. After all, I had only two clients to start out with. But I knew God wanted me at home so we took the leap of faith. Sure enough, after some marketing and spreading the word, the phone started ringing!

I feel so blessed and thankful when I look at how God brought me full circle -- from freelancing to working full time and then back home again to freelance. He is so good!

Just as God provided me with good things in His timing, He wants to do the same for you! Just remember these two verses:

Matthew 6:33 -- "But seek ye first the kingdom of God and his righteousness; and all these things shall be added unto you."

Matthew 7:11 -- "How much more shall your Heavenly Father give good things to them that ask?"

Chapter Ten

"Having Done All To Stand, Stand!"
Ephesians 6:13-14

There's probably nothing more frustrating or bewildering in the process of recovering from anxiety and panic than feeling the sudden onset of symptoms after a long period without them. Just as cancer can go into remission and then resurface, panic symptoms can go into remission and then resurface again, much to the sufferer's amazement. This resurfacing of symptoms is known as a setback and is common among individuals learning to cope with anxiety and panic disorder.

Quite often, a person will say these returning symptoms did so for no apparent reason. Actually, that may be the case. The victim may not have been anxious consciously or even subconsciously. However, your body's past reactions have prepared it to respond improperly to even the slightest stimulus. But there are ways to keep the body from reacting this way and to keep the setbacks from being so frequent.

The first step in successfully overcoming a setback is the same as the first "Step to Triumphant Living:" Acceptance. It is critical that you accept all the symptoms no matter what. Whether they are "out of the blue" or whether you can identify a specific stressor, you need to give yourself permission to feel this way. Once again, don't "fuel the fire" by reacting with an "Oh my!" If you do, you may find yourself in the midst of a full-blown panic attack instead of simply handling some mild symptoms. Acceptance and keeping yourself from becoming upset by whatever your body throws at you will make whatever setbacks you have fewer and farther between.

The second step in overcoming a setback is to relearn and practice your coping skills and "Steps to Triumphant Living." You will find that often the symptoms have much greater intensity after you've gone for a long period of time without experiencing them. It is natural to be caught off-guard and have the need to brush up on these skills and techniques. Once again, be patient with yourself and don't be alarmed...you will feel well again.

Third, practice your positive self-talk and scripture recitation and meditation to overcome negative thoughts. It is important not to let satan discourage you by bringing up the past. When he does remind you of the past, you remind him of his future! And while you are at it, encourage yourself by looking at how far you've come.

Fourth, you may need to visit your doctor for some additional therapy or perhaps even an increase in medication to help you get through the setback. The need to do so will most likely be determined by the duration of the setback. Sometimes it will last for a day or two and other times for a period of a week or more. Nonetheless, do not be discouraged if you need additional counseling or medication to get you over the hump -- it doesn't mean that you are weak or that no progress has been made. It simply means that this time you need a little extra push.

I experienced setbacks several times during the past nine years. Some of them were "out of the blue," but most I could attribute to the fact that I was beginning to commit to too many activities. Either I would take on too many projects with simultaneous deadlines or I would schedule too many meetings or appointments for the same week. In any case, there were times that I needed to schedule an "emergency" doctor's appointment. But I

81

always managed to work my way through and overcome the symptoms once more. The illness never regressed to the point that I had to "start all over again." Instead, the setback was simply a reminder of what I dealt with and a message to cut back on my activities and commitments.

One final thought brings me back to the scripture in the title of this chapter, Ephesians 6:13-14 -- "Having done all to stand, Stand." In other words, when you have done all you know to do and you haven't the energy to do anything more, just stand. Hold on to the word of God and simply let time pass. Sometimes that is all you can do, but be assured, "This, too, shall pass."

Chapter Eleven

"Children Are An Heritage Of The Lord"
Psalms 127:3

Randy and I decided after we were married for about a year and a half to start a family of our own. Little did we know that, too, would be no simple task. After about 10 months of trying, I made an appointment with my doctor to see if there were any indications that we wouldn't be able to have children. He ran some simple tests and after all was determined to be okay, he decided to proceed with a laparoscopy. So we scheduled that minor surgery and found that I had endometriosis, a common problem where the lining of the uterus grows in abnormal locations. The endometriosis was removed with a laser and I was told there should be no problems with having children.

Now a part of me thought that the reason I hadn't conceived up to this point was because God was watching out for me and knew that I couldn't handle being pregnant. The thinking behind this was that I was on medication for panic disorder and if I were to become pregnant, I would have to get off the Klonopin. And that thought scared me! I also knew that at times it was all I could do to take care of my husband, myself and our two dogs. Why would I want to further complicate my life with a baby? But I knew what the Bible said about children and that they are an heritage of the Lord and a blessing, so I prayed and turned the whole thing over to God. I figured if He wanted me to have children, He would give me the strength to get through the pregnancy and beyond.

During this time I was led to Samuel 1 where Hannah had wanted to bear children. After reading about how Hannah asked the Lord for a child, I decided that was what I would do. I prayed that if it was His will for me to have a child, then let it be so.

Well, it must have been the Lord's will because after only two months of trying, I was pregnant. Immediately upon finding out the good news, I made a call to Dr. Babai to find out the steps necessary for getting off Klonopin. His instructions were to taper down the doses over a five-day period. At that point, I would be completely off, taking only the Norpramin for the remainder of the pregnancy.

Anyone using antianxiety medication might be able to relate to the fear I was tempted to feel knowing I had to get off a medication I had been taking for four years. But it was a necessity because Klonopin is known to interfere with the developing baby's heart formation. I am thankful that Norpramin is safe to take, though, because at least it would help with the symptoms should they return.

I followed Dr.Babai's instructions for eliminating the use of Klonopin and I did feel a bit anxious while doing so. I just made certain I was exercising and eating right in order to do what I could naturally to help keep from being so sensitized. I also gave myself time for extra rest and for practicing the relaxation techniques to keep my body as calm as possible.

The first few days weren't too bad. Some of the medication must have been left in my system. But the third day of being entirely off Klonopin was the worst! Many symptoms that I hadn't felt in more than a year returned with such great force that it took me by surprise. One of the reasons, I'm sure, that they were so strong was that this was also the evening of a fund-raising event I organized for a professional organization. It was poor timing on my part to have this event coincide with my first week off the medication, but I wanted to get off the drug as soon as possible for the baby's sake. I remember feeling so "floaty" and "cloudy" as a result of all the adrenaline in my system. I could barely concentrate to eat my dinner or speak in front of those in attendance. But somehow I managed to get through the event and home safely. I thought the symptoms would subside upon arriving home. But as I lay in bed, they increased in intensity to the point that I experienced a full-blown panic attack for the first time since 1988. I had the sensation that my brain was flying apart. I was trembling, my outer extremities were tingling, my heart was racing and I was sweating. I remember thinking, "Oh, no, I can't possibly deal with this for nine months!"

So I got up and took a Klonopin tablet to stop the symptoms in order to sleep. I felt so guilty for doing so, but I figured one tablet wasn't going to create a heart deformity in my baby. I would call Dr. Babai the next day.

After speaking with the doctor and relating the previous night's activities, he instructed me to take a Klonopin every now and then if I needed it in case of an emergency. My OB-GYN doctor agreed and said to avoid it if possible, but a little bit here and there probably wouldn't hurt anything. It was such a relief just to know that I could take it if I had to!

When I spoke to my father about having a full-blown panic attack for the first time since 1988, he immediately went into prayer and put Matthew 18:19-20 to work. He prayed the prayer of agreement with me believing I would no longer need the medication. He made a note of it in his Bible, dated it, and asked the Lord to keep me and the baby from harm. Much to my amazement, I did not need the medication, nor did I experience anything but mild symptoms from that day forward. God is so good!

I didn't have panic symptoms, thank God, but I sure did experience some of the other intense side effects of pregnancy --

like morning sickness. Now morning sickness isn't just limited to morning, I can attest to that. I was sick all the time! At first I could control the nausea and vomiting by eating, would you believe, Smarties candies? I never went anywhere without them! But as the weeks went on, the nausea and vomiting became unbearable. I had become dehydrated and required a homecare nurse to put me on intravenous fluid for several days. I was also given Phenergan tablets, the same thing I used to take when I suffered from nausea and vomiting due to anxiety and panic, to control the morning sickness. After a few days I was much better and took the Phenergan faithfully every four to six hours. Over the next few months, I did very well.

It was interesting to learn that Phenergan is actually a sedative that relaxes the body. I couldn't help but think that maybe the Lord had orchestrated events such that I could trade in the Klonopin, which was not safe to take, for the Phenergan, which was safe, during my pregnancy to produce the same desired calmness. He never ceases to amaze me by taking care of everything!

During my pregnancy I wasn't able to work as much as I had been because I was so sick. I also had to take care of myself so as not to get too busy and overwhelmed. Prior to becoming pregnant, I had been working for several clients in the Akron-Canton area and putting in a pretty full schedule. But my strength was not what it had been and I found myself cutting back and looking for work closer to home or work that wouldn't require leaving home at all. It just so happened that my father's real estate and appraisal business was booming and he needed someone to help him set up an office outside his house. Another client only three miles away popped up out of nowhere. So these two pieces of business kept me just busy enough to provide the extra income we needed without taking a toll on me physically. Didn't I tell you God takes care of everything?

Things were going fine until the seventh month of my

pregnancy. The morning sickness returned with increased intensity and along with it came a new symptom: swelling. And I mean balloon-style! I filled up with so much water that at times I could not put shoes on. But my blood pressure was normal so there was no indication that I had toxemia, which is sometimes seen in first pregnancies and characterized by severe swelling. So I just tried to watch my salt intake and keep my feet elevated.

At the beginning of the eighth month, the pregnancy took yet another twist: I started having contractions that were three minutes apart the evening after our baby shower. I thank God we were able to get our birthing classes in right under the wire, too, or I wouldn't have known to call the doctor and get to the hospital.

After spending half a day on the maternity floor, I was released and put on medication to stop the pre-term labor. I was also given instructions to take it easy and to cease attending my prenatal aerobics class.

For the next four weeks I was absolutely miserable. The swelling continued to worsen and the medication I was on made me feel strange. I think one of the women at church could tell how miserable I was because she came up to me with a scripture that the Lord had given her during her pregnancy. It was 1 Timothy 2:15 -- ''Not withstanding she shall be saved in childbearing if they continue in faith and charity and holiness with sobriety.'' It brought tears to my eyes then and still does because that verse came to mean a lot to me -- how wonderful that the Lord directed a verse specifically to pregnant women!

Little did I know that very evening I would stand on that verse. After vomiting profusely I looked in the mirror and my face was all puffy and distorted. My eyes had swollen shut and my hearing was also affected. I told my husband we needed to get to the hospital immediately -- something was wrong.

Well, come to find out I did indeed have toxemia. The protein levels in the urine indicated such, but my blood pressure never did go up. The contractions started up again while I was at the hospital and I began to dilate. But this time they didn't try to stop labor from progressing. We would be delivering our son soon -- four weeks early.

After 22-1/2 hours of labor, the doctor was finally able to bring "Little Luke" into the world with the help of forceps. Randy and I, both exhausted from lack of sleep, were so relieved that the whole ordeal was over! But another ordeal was just beginning. It started when we heard a nurse call out to my doctor, "Was this baby's cord wrapped around his neck?" Immediately we knew something was going on. And we didn't hear our son cry. Instead he just whimpered and then did nothing. Randy and I grabbed each other's hands and agreed that Luke would be fine. We prayed that God would correct whatever was wrong and keep our boy from harm. Then the doctors and nurses carried him off to the Neonatal Intensive Care Unit (NICU) for observation and tests. After about two hours, the doctors came into my room and all I remember was the Indian neonatologist saying, "Baby very sick." Luke was having severe respiratory problems and would be put on a ventilator and oxygen. Apparently his lungs were not fully developed and he was experiencing respiratory distress syndrome -- something common in premature babies. But Randy, my mom, dad and I, immediately prayed again that the Lord would heal our son.

The next few days while I was recovering from the toxemia and delivery, we visited Luke in the NICU and watched him fight for his life. It was so hard to see him with the ventilator in his mouth and all the other tubes and wires that were monitoring his vital signs and giving him nourishment. It was apparent he wouldn't be coming home with us for some time.

For the next three weeks we went back and forth to the hospital twice each day to visit our son. Everyone at our church was praying for him to overcome this rough start to life and begin breathing on his own in "room air." He would make a little progress each day, and we found ourselves having to practice making positive faith-filled statements and speaking life over our boy. Each time a negative report would come forth, we would have to trust the Lord and say to ourselves, "Whose report are we going to believe? We shall believe the report of the Lord!" It seemed as though we would cross one hurdle and then the doctors would find something else over which to have us worry.

I'll never forget the afternoon when I spoke with the doctor who said they were going to run some more tests on Luke because he was a "floppy baby." In medical terms this meant he had hypotonia or decreased muscle tone. They also said he had a feeble cry. They were going to do an MRI and a chromosome analysis, among other tests. After putting two and two together I realized they were checking for birth defects or cerebral palsy or some other disorder that may cause hypotonia.

Of course I knew the doctors and nurses had to investigate anything suspicious and they were doing a fantastic job. But it was hard not to let fear or doubt or unbelief enter the picture. When it is your own child that's a big challenge. And for Luke's sake we couldn't allow ourselves the luxury of worry or fear. This was a war against the enemy and we prayed like never before. We pleaded the blood of Jesus over our son and claimed that Jesus' name was above every name -- and that included hypotonia and whatever was at the root of the problem. In the meantime the Lord told me to shut my mouth. He wouldn't even let me speak the words cerebral palsy or mental retardation or brain damage even though I knew that was what the doctors were looking for. Instead, I was to speak only positive faith-filled words like, "God is good all the time." "Our boy is whole from the top of his head to the soles of his feet." "Luke is healed."

Those three weeks put our beliefs to the test. Did we really believe the things we said about our faith and our God? Would our belief system withstand the storms of life or crack under the pres-

sure? Well, we stood on the word and worshipped the Lord with
our lips. Like our pastor always says -- "You can worship your
way through anything!" And he was right. He also said to "Let the
doctors do their best and God will do the rest!" So that is what we
did.

Slowly but surely, Luke's muscle tone began to improve
and one by one the test results came back fine. Finally, the day
arrived that Luke was allowed to come home. We shed tears as we
walked out of that NICU, but they were tears of joy and victory.
Our boy was healed and he was a big, healthy 8 lbs. 1 oz. when he
left. He was eating and sleeping and crying just like any normal
newborn. And let me tell you, there was no concern over a feeble
cry after he got home -- he exercised those lungs quite well!

The first few days that our "miracle boy" was home were
the longest days of our lives. It was one big blur of diaper changing
and feeding and bottle-making...all without much sleep. I wondered
what I had gotten myself into! I was so thankful that while Luke
was in the hospital, I had a chance to recover and get much-needed
rest. I don't know how new moms do it when they bring their
newborns home a day or two after delivery! I realized I had found
another way that what satan meant for evil with Luke's illness, God
turned to good with a miracle healing and a chance for mom to
recover.

Even though I'd had three weeks of uninterrupted sleep at
night, I was still fatigued and overwhelmed with my new son. One
of those days when I was very stressed, my sister watched my son
and I had lunch with Randy. On the way back I heard a radio
program in which a local pastor, Joey Johnson of The House of the
Lord in Akron, was teaching on the verse 1 Timothy 2:15. That
was the same verse the lady at church had given me to hold onto
during my time in the hospital. But he was looking at it in a way I'd
never heard before. He said the verse says a woman "shall be saved
in childbearing" if she continues in faith and charity and holiness

with sobriety. He explained that the word "saved" here doesn't mean "salvation" but instead "fulfillment." In other words, a woman shall be fulfilled with giving birth to a child. But the key word here is the last part -- if she continues in faith and charity and holiness with sobriety. And this pastor said that she will be fulfilled *if* she doesn't get hooked into the world's system that says she must have a career and an important title and a big salary in order to be fulfilled. Instead, if she keeps her focus on her faith in the Lord and in her job as a mother, she can find all the fulfillment she needs.

This teaching comforted me so much that afternoon and was exactly what I needed to hear. And from that day forward I have asked God each morning for the strength to get me through the day and to be able to accomplish the tasks that are set before me. And each day, He does.

Chapter Twelve

"And The Truth Shall Make You Free"
John 8:32

Some of you may be beginning this chapter thinking, "Okay, I'm in the last chapter of the book, now when is she going to tell me how to overcome anxiety and panic?" The truth is, I already have. But I felt the same way you do back when I was learning about the disorder. After reading each book I would feel like the author really didn't tell me, step by step, how I was to get rid of this illness. But in all actuality, I have related the only cure for anxiety and panic disorder. It is not a step-by-step process, as some may think. Though you can take steps to overcome the illness, they occur in no sequential order, just as the symptoms occur in no specific order.

Instead, overcoming panic and anxiety is a process of combining several things -- medication, psychotherapy, education about the illness, and the series of coping skills and steps that were discussed in Chapter Four. It is a process of changing your behavior and reactions to life's events. And it is a process of changing the way you speak and think. But above all it takes time.

Looking back at myself in 1988 and then looking at the way I am now, I see that the last nine years have been a gradual metamorphosis into a different person. I've had to learn about myself and the illness I deal with, learn the skills and steps to cope with and overcome it, and change my behavior, reactions, speaking and thinking.

The steps and coping skills I have outlined for you in this book, combined with the powerful word of God, really do work to overcome anxiety and panic disorder. I am a walking example of this. Think about it...during a three-year period I went through getting a difficult divorce, moving, buying a house, finding out my husband cheated on me, getting remarried, undergoing surgery, switching medication and doctors...all with only minor symptoms of panic. Then, I experienced a death in the family, a serious illness with Randy, another surgery, nine Dalmatians in the house at once, two job changes, going off antianxiety medication, a difficult pregnancy, childbirth and a seriously-ill newborn...all with only one full-blown panic attack. I'd say those are pretty good results!

I remember when a friend of mine "after the illness" ran into my high school basketball coach who knew me "before the illness." She mentioned she was an acquaintance of mine and the coach replied something like, "Well, at least you always know where you stand with Angela -- she's rather outspoken." My friend replied, "No, actually, Angela is kind of quiet." To which the coach said, "Not the Angela I know!"

Another friend described me as "rather laid back." No one would have said that prior to 1988. But it took time, not to mention prayer, to get from then to now. And so it will with you take time, strength, courage and prayer, to get on the road to recovery.

When I reflect on the path I have traveled, I also find myself asking, "What did I learn from this experience?" "What did I gain from having suffered with anxiety and panic?" My answer to that would be two-fold: I learned humility and strength.

The humility was learned in that I now know beyond the shadow of a doubt that I can do nothing without the Lord Jesus Christ. Prior to 1988, I was of the notion that everything I did was of my own accord. If something happened it was because I made it happen and I was proud of it. If it didn't happen, I would just have to try harder the next time to see that it did. But through suffering from anxiety and panic, I realize that something as simple as getting out of bed in the morning is a gift from God. And it is funny, but I don't have to try as hard to accomplish things. With God working through me, it seems that He allows me to get the job done more quickly than if I were trying to do it on my own. I find I have more time even though I am tending to many more tasks. It is like Proverbs 3:16 says, "Length of days is in her right hand."

As for strength, overcoming anxiety and panic disorder was the most difficult thing I ever went through. I feel that if I have the strength to make it through that, I have the strength to make it through anything. As Dr. James Dobson says in his book, *When God Doesn't Make Sense*, "adversity builds toughness." Because I came through that difficult challenge still standing, I now have a certain resilience that says "anything else is going to be a cinch." I feel it prepared me for the challenging times ahead: my divorce, the death of my mother-in-law, the difficult pregnancy and birth of my son. It wasn't easy to get through those situations, but at least I knew that with God, I had the strength to rise above them.

And it will be that way for you, too. There aren't many things more difficult than overcoming a mental or emotional illness. And when you make it through, you, too, will feel that with God on your side there is no curve ball life can throw that you can't handle.

You may be in the midst of some of your worst panic or anxious episodes right now and may disagree with my saying that you will be a stronger person because of it. I also felt that way at one point. Back when I was barely able to go out of the apartment to go to the grocery store, no one could have convinced me that one day I would be living a joyful, victorious life. But it sure is true today and I have even gone one step beyond that to accomplish things I never thought possible or even remotely considered. For instance, just this past year I have embarked upon the elected office of president for a local chapter of an organization of women in the field of communications. I would have never felt that I was qualified or confident enough to handle something like that even five or six years ago. And no one could have gotten me to believe that I would write a book telling others how to overcome anxiety and panic back when I was in the midst of my most major symptoms. But it has all happened one step at a time!

I still cope with symptoms occasionally when I forget and get too many things going at once. Sometimes I even experience symptoms for no apparent reason. But I try not to get alarmed by them because that will only make things worse. For the most part I simply see my doctor four times a year for medicine reviews as required by our insurance. To this point I have not had to begin taking Klonopin again (another miracle!), which I thought I would have to do soon after the birth of our son. Now my condition is being controlled medicine-wise only by Norpramin. The rest is done by God and me.

I look forward to working at home doing freelance writing and editing for whatever clients come my way. But my biggest job is taking care of our son, Luke. The Lord has provided for us so I can stay home and make the transition to a full-time wife and mother. That may just prove to be my most challenging role yet!

One final thought...my father brought to my attention recently that miracles do not produce faith. If they did, every one of the Jews would have believed in and trusted God when He parted the Red Sea, rained manna from Heaven and watched over them in many other ways on their journey to the Promised Land. But they didn't. They griped and complained and had to wander in the desert for 40 years. Instead, it is the other way around. The truth is that faith produces miracles. And I've lived to see that statement proved true in my healing, my son's healing and in countless other situations. My prayer is that your faith will produce a miracle for you and that you will be free from anxiety and panic and move on to triumphant and joyful living in Jesus Christ.

A Sinner's Prayer

To Receive Jesus Christ as Savior

Dear Heavenly Father,

I come to you in the name of Jesus and I am so sorry that I have grieved you. I know that I am a sinner and that your Son died on the cross for me so that I might have eternal life in heaven with You. I know that I must be saved or "born again" in order to come to heaven with You when I die. Your word says so in John 3:3. So now I ask You to come into my heart and live big in me. I ask you to be Lord of my life and help me to be what you want me to be.

Your word also says "...with the heart man believeth unto righteousness; and with the mouth confession is made unto salvation" (Romans 10:10). I do believe with my heart and I confess Jesus now as my Lord. Therefore, I am saved!

Thank you, Father!

Signed_____

Date_____

Bibliography

ANXIETY AND PANIC ATTACKS: THEIR CAUSE AND
CURE by Robert Handly with Pauline Neff. New York: Fawcett
Crest, 1985.

FROM PANIC TO POWER, by Lucinda Bassett. New York:
HarperCollins, 1995.

LOVE MUST BE TOUGH, by Dr. James C. Dobson. Dallas:Word
Publishing, 1983.

PANIC DISORDER (pamphlet), American Psychiatric Association.
Washington, D.C.:APA Joint Commission on Public Affiars and the
Division of Public Affairs, 1989.

PEACE FROM NERVOUS SUFFERING by Dr. Claire Weekes.
New York: Bantam Books, 1972.

WEBSTER'S NEW WORLD DICTIONARY. New York: Prentice
Hall Press, 1986.

WHEN GOD DOESN'T MAKE SENSE by Dr. James C. Dobson.
Wheaton, IL: Tyndale House, 1993.

Index

Order Form

Check your bookstore or order directly from us.

Please send me _____ copies of *Don't Forget To Look Up:*
A Christian's Guide to Overcoming Anxiety and Panic Attacks.
Copies are $10.95 each plus $3.00 each for shipping and handling.
Number of Books Ordered_____ x $10.95 = _____
Shipping & Handling $3.00 x # books ordered = _____
Ohio Sales Tax (OH residents only)
.63 x # books ordered = _____
Total = _____

Enclosed is a check or money order for the appropriate amount.

Send Book(s) to:
Name_____
Address_____
City_____State_____ Zip_____

Mail order form and make check payable to:
Brittain Communications
P.O. Box 2567
North Canton, OH 44720

* See the following page for the new *Don't Forget To Look Up* Workbook and Discussion Questions.

New! Workbook & Discussion Questions

Order your copy now! *Don't Forget To Look Up Workbook & Discussion Questions.* This handbook is for individuals, groups and group leaders who want to work through and overcome panic disorder. Created to be used following each of the 12 chapters of *Don't Forget To Look Up*, the discussion questions cause one to think and reflect on the ideas and principles that he or she has just read. It also helps to reinforce the coping skills and strategies to overcome panic disorder and create a more personalized road to recovery.

Please send me _____ copies of the *Don't Forget To Look Up Workbook and Discussion Questions.* Copies are $3.95 each plus $2.50 each for shipping and handling.

Number of Workbooks Ordered_____ x $3.95 = _____

Shipping & Handling $2.50 x # books ordered   = _____

Ohio Sales Tax (OH residents only)

                           .21 x # books ordered   = _____

                                  Total   = _____

Enclosed is a check or money order for the appropriate amount.

Send Book(s) to:

Name_____

Address_____

City_____State_____ Zip_____

Mail order form and make check payable to:
           Brittain Communications
           P.O. Box 2567
           North Canton, OH 44720

Afterword

It is hard to believe it has been four years since "Don't Forget To Look Up" was originally published. I remember thinking once we had the books in hand, "Okay, God, we've got the books, this is great, now we're done." He said to me, "No, you are just getting started." And of course, He was right. We then went on to facilitate a support group, produce a workbook to accompany the title, and develop a website, all while continuing to minister to many people.

Through this ministry, God is continually teaching me things about myself and about anxiety and panic disorder. One of the most important things that I have learned upon overcoming the acute stage of the illness is that panic will try to rear its ugly head time and time again. Once you are beyond the daily or even weekly panic attacks and you have reclaimed your life and health, the fear will try to come back and reclaim the territory it once had. But you can't let that happen! One of the ways I believe the enemy tries to get us to regress is to get us overcommitted and stressed out once again with too much on our "to do" list. Once we are feeling "normal" and confident again, we have a tendency to fill up our schedule and get right back to the Type A trap and create the environment for the symptoms to begin again. God has shown me that with this type of disorder, you have to constantly be aware that you have a tendency to slip into old bad habits. You have to realize that you need to be proactive and pace yourself or you very well could begin to experience symptoms once again. I like what Dr. Archibald Hart says: We need to treat life like a marathon and not a sprint or we will give out half-way through the race.

During the past several years my husband, son and I have faced various struggles and challenges...because life happens! At times symptoms would begin to surface again, but praise God I am aware of the signs and know how to take the actions I need to keep from taking any steps backward.

106

Most importantly, I have learned that overcoming anxiety and panic attacks is as much a spiritual battle as it is a physical battle. "For we wrestle not against flesh and blood, but against principalities, against powers, against rulers of the darkness of this world, against spiritual wickedness in high places" (Eph. 6:12). The enemy uses stress to keep us in fear and bondage so we cannot further God's kingdom here on earth. But Jesus can show us our limits and boundaries, teach us to prioritize so that we can find the pace that is right for us, the pace that we're most productive at, and the pace at which we serve Him most effectively. That way we can accomplish what He wants us to accomplish for His kingdom...and that is what it is all about!